THE HOUSE THAT NAMUH BUILT

By

Renford

ISBN: 0-7596-5543-X

This book is printed on acid free paper.

First published by IAMPRESS.

1stBooks - rev. 3/19/02

Perfection

Formed in perfection, a part of Universal Being, perfection is our birthright. Perfectly created, still we display imperfection everywhere and in every way. Understanding these imperfections is of critical importance. We have the potential for ultimate perfection whether in this life or one to come. We cannot in the beginning know all and should certainly avoid being a know-it-all. Perfection is about constructive thought and begins with self-observation. Complete and full awareness of all begins with awareness and knowledge of Self.

Knowing Self is the process of knowing God, and all of our work is on Self.

When one denies imperfections in one's conscious self, one denies the process of perfection. How can one work effectively on Self and deny the problem? How can one evolve and unfold and at the same time deny the very imperfections that keep one from perfection? How can one gain understanding without peace? How can one have peace without harmony? How can harmony be achieved by denying imperfections? Where does one begin but with the observation of Self? The constant eye on Self reveals all. It is no one else's job, and the benefits accrue to no one else. It is enough initially to recognize what is happening as it happens, to be aware consciously when illustrating lack of control.

We watch the Self, refusing to be complacent in the good times and refusing to lose faith in the potential of Self in difficult times. The search for knowledge of Self is the desire to come to knowing. It is not a search for spiritual concrete or absolute assurances. Human absolutes are fixed ideas, codes and dogmas all frozen in time. They are the headstones in the cemetery of the spiritually dead. All are imperfect and fail is a mantra for failure. Why should one abandon the search for perfection? It is this process that is necessary for unfoldment. When the focus is on our vision of wholeness and harmony in the Self, there is no room for judgmental thoughts with regard to the imperfections of others.

Our actions are seen by others and are important, but what we are, what we have discovered of the Self, is more important. To know the difference between action and knowledge of Self is important because future actions will be controlled only by knowledge of Self. Only awareness of the imperfections we have created from perfection can possibly lead us to the pure potentiality of our being - perfection.

This is taken from *"In Search of Self"* by Renford

ACKNOWLEDGEMENTS

Regardless of latter day influences I would be remiss not to mention those who have encouraged me to take responsibility for myself. My parents deserve the credit for this. They had nothing to do with the conclusions drawn from my studies but a great deal to with the consciousness to study.

There have been a number of contributors to this work but my wife, Diane, has been, in the final analysis, the one who has contributed most to making my work readable.

Both of my daughters, Dawn-Renee and Jade, have contributed by reading and critiquing. They have made suggestions that have helped in my efforts to write so that anyone can understand on some level the Universal Laws

Teachers

The three teachers who stand out in my mind are Arthur Tunnel, Tajwar Shadikhan, and Nana K. Bonze. Art Tunnel was my first business employer and mentor. Tajwar became a partner in a business I founded in Hong Kong, and Nana at that time was an employee of UNESCO in Bahrain.

Contributors

My subject matter has come from my own search for understanding and has not been taken from a particular individual, philosophy or religion.

The following individuals have contributed either through discussions, suggested books, editing or proof reading.

Diane Powell, Dawn-Renee Powell Weatherford, Jade Powell, James Powell III, Marina Foster, Ronnie Dickerson, Lee Saunders, Bill Brown, Ronna Zinn, Debbie Volneck, Wesley Boshell, and Kevin McKeon.

Paintings and Illustrations

The cover for this book was painted by Jennifer Zinn and the layout was the work of Bill Cooper.

CONTENTS

INTRODUCTION

I began writing this book in 1988. Initially, I was using the idea of a silo to explain the levels of the mind. It was very short and was intended as a tract or brief for introducing such studies. In time, I began to develop the story with the idea of producing a book for children that could be used to introduce the Universal Principles. Obviously, I could not leave this idea alone and kept coming back to it with new ideas. Over the ten years of its production, there have been many layers. I have taken it a bit far for younger children, but certainly a parent who understands how important these principles are can use it for instruction.

I am told that few allegories are written any more, but for a basic introduction to the Universal Laws and to the course of study provided by the Institute of Applied Metaphysics, I believe this format will provide some examples of how the Universal Laws work. More importantly, it leads directly into the study of the Laws, which are no less than the very Laws of Life.

This story is about one man's Self-discovery, a common man who was doing some uncommon thinking. There are many events in this story, but they primarily provide the background for the evolution of his thinking. *For this reason, Namuh's thoughts are recorded in script.*

This is not a new story in the sense that there are none in our world who experience Self-discovery. There have been those we revere as Great Masters who have made such discoveries and taught us the Universal Laws so that all may come to understanding.

Rarely in our ancient texts is the process of self-discovery revealed. One day a man is a prince, and the next he renounces it all to go in the great search of Self-knowledge, as was the case with the Buddha. One day Jesus is the son of a carpenter working with his father, and the next time we see him, he is already attracting a following. We are left to believe or disbelieve that their revelation and Self-discovery were due to divine process because they were special messengers from God or themselves gods.

The lives and the process of the evolvement of such people are often clouded by events, major historical occurrences or the legends developed by their followers. What we have recorded are often embellished stories designed to impress those for whom the texts were meant to attract. The more prominent of these teachers are revered today as founders of the world's great religions.

The discovery of knowledge, power and the development of man's thinking is always exciting. So come to the Valley of the Nam and follow the story of Namuh. Maybe, if you are attentive, you will make discoveries for yourself as we follow Namuh's journey in the mind.

CHAPTER ONE

THE VALLEY OF THE NAM

The valley of the Nam was like a world unto itself, a garden in the midst of mountain ranges. There was an abundance of all the people of Nam could want. No Nam went hungry because of a lack of crop production, and all were employed, communal fashion, in this effort. Regardless of any additional skills they might have, this was the primary activity of the Nam people. Even the Crew Elders who were considered the chosen of God, and who enjoyed many privileges, also participated in the production of Egdelwonk, or "Wonk" for short, their staple crop. While everyone enjoyed abundance at harvest time, their fear was of the extremely harsh winters, which annually ravaged the valley.

Wonk mixed with Feileb, the main garden vegetable of the people of Nam, constituted the most desirable meal. The problem was that it was often only one or the other that was available at the same time. At harvest time, there was more than enough Wonk, but Feileb would be out of season. There was something about having both together that produced a state of contentment and happiness. The Nam people called this state Modsiw, or "Mod" for short.

A common greeting was "May your house be filled with Mod". The answer was typically, "And may you never be without Mod". This was a carry over from the time when the ancient god Efil had been worshipped. Since Wonk was necessary to life, it became the central focus for the people of Nam.

Wonk was a communal produce raised by the whole Nam community, but Feileb was a vegetable that each family had to raise in its own garden if they were to have it at all. It was,

1

therefore, the objective of each family to raise enough Feileb to last as long as there was Wonk. This was the world of the Nam.

No one had successfully left the valley to later come back and tell the people about another world. Some had left in search of adventure and some to escape work or punishment, but those who did return only reported mountains in every direction. Those who had not returned were presumed dead. They had been unable to penetrate what was said to be an endless range of mountains inhabited by fierce beasts. The Valley of Nam was the only valley that could sustain life. If they managed to get through the smaller ranges, they found themselves facing ever more lofty peaks covered with ice and snow even in the summer months.

The highest mountains that locked them in their valley appeared to have no passes through which a single climber could go, much less animals. They were impassable unless a route through them was discovered, and none had been. For the Nam, all that existed surrounding the valley was the perilous world of rock, ice and snow.

There was no way to know what, if anything else, might exist. They saw the mountains much the way many today view space and our universe. To them, the rest of the earth did not exist. In fact, the Nam had given up because they could see no purpose in searching for something that for them did not exist.

All this changed with the arrival of the Great God Pilot. He told them of other valleys and promised that he would return and take them to a valley with no winters. To the Nam, this was a wonderful vision and made the search for a way out even less important. They had given up because they did not believe there was life outside the valley. It was unnecessary now to search for a way out because their God would return and take them out. Pilot had answered this question of what was outside the Valley of Nam and the mountains that surrounded the valley. He had also provided the solution. All they had to do was be faithful to him and everything would be all right.

All any Nam knew of such things was to be found in the teachings of their priests, the Crew Elders. The Crew Elders also taught them of Missile, The Evil One, and there was an image of him that some said had been left by the Great God Pilot. Pilot had said that if they did not obey Him, Missile would kill everyone. The Nam understood Missile to be a bad god but had no understanding of evil as a concept. Missile was an enemy of Pilot, but apparently Missile could be commanded to do Pilot's bidding.

Pilot, being the only power they knew, must have originated their existence. They were taught that Efil had been their god when they had been filled with superstition, but Pilot had proved himself to be the most powerful. He was simply the Lord of all and reigned somewhere outside the Valley of the Nam.

The Nam concept of life was simple. Their priest taught that the elements had their kingdom, the animals their kingdom and the Nam had their kingdom. The Nam ruled over the other two kingdoms and could do as they liked with them. There was little concept of the power of the mind or its dimensions. Even Pilot and the Law of the Log, his words which had been left for them to live by, made no mention of anything or any power within the Nam that made them special.

They knew virtually nothing about the workings of the mind. There was little inkling for them of its creative powers. Intuitive thought and imagination were not well developed in the Nam. The few who had demonstrated such powers were suspect, and any child exhibiting these tendencies was severely punished. Any attempt to learn about this faculty was frowned upon by the priest who governed the Nam. There had been one who had taught the Nam of such things, but he had been banished from the valley by the Crew Elders.

This story is about Self-discovery. It is the awakening of first one Nam called Namuh, and then a growing body of individuals to a knowledge almost extinct in the valley. For the priest, this knowledge was the work of Missile, The Evil One, who had visited destruction on the valley in their ancient past.

Any individual thought that went outside the bounds of their laws and traditions was dangerous, and the priests' duty was to protect the people from themselves.

The teacher, Renni Nam, who had talked about the power of the mind, was considered a blasphemer against the Great God Pilot, so no one ever spoke of him or referred to his teachings. The Nam were afraid that should they even discuss such matters, they too would be banished. There was one mind that simply could not accept these limitations. We call him Namuh.

CHAPTER TWO

NAMUH

Namuh was, like everyone else in the Valley of the Nam, a farmer. Even the skilled tradesmen and priests farmed. Little time was given to the frivolous and celebration was limited to one occasion, the Great Harvest Feast. All had to work in the fields, especially at harvest time. The Valley of Nam was fertile, and the harvests were bountiful, however, the winters could be long and harsh. Many winters were so severe that survival was in the balance, and starvation was not unknown.

During the winter two years before this story, the Nam had to slaughter much of their live- stock because many had used up their allotment of Wonk. To the Nam, this was almost like cannibalism because they rarely ate domesticated animals. Their sheep provided wool and the cattle their dairy products. The only meat they had was what hunters brought in from the mountains, and that was only for the Harvest Feast once a year.

They faced the specter of starvation that year like no other in memory, but Pilot had saved them. The early spring He had sent was the salvation that they had prayed for. The Crew Elders had told them that the Great God Pilot had heard their prayers and knew of their tribulations. He alone could have saved them and did so because of their adherence to the Law of the Log, the written law he had left for them.

There had been plenty of Wonk at harvest time, and their seasonal vegetable Feileb was a matter of how much each Nam family planted. However, because of their reliance only on tradition and the restrictive teachings of the Crew Elders, there had been little advancement in planning and distribution. This was not something with which the Nam were to concern themselves because Pilot would take care of them. Only the

Crew Elders knew the will of the Great God Pilot, and they insisted on adherence to the Law of the Log. If there was wastage of their resources, it was the will of Pilot.

Preparation was simply not understood in the manner that we understand it today. Each Nam family was allotted its share of Wonk, but during the winter just past, there had not been enough to feed the stock when they most needed it. It always seemed to be feast or famine. At harvest time, there was far more than could be eaten or prepared for the animals, yet there was no main system for storage. Each Nam family received a portion of the harvest to sustain itself, but there was little in the way of storage facilities constructed by each family. It was thought to be a sign of insufficient faith in Pilot.

All the Nam looked to the Crew Elders for direction as only they could establish a program affecting the people of Nam. Without their specific direction, nothing could be independently undertaken by the Nam people. Even the King and Queen dared not be so presumptuous as to suggest that they knew better than Pilot, and if Pilot wanted something planned, He would tell the Crew Elders.

Everyone, including the Crew Elders was aware of the problem, but they were all looking to the Navigator, (Chief Priest), Worran, for a revelation from Pilot. Privately, among their immediate families, many of the Nam voiced their dissatisfaction but no one spoke publicly and no one acted. They were too busy complaining about the harshness of the winter weather to look for solutions to the problem.

Namuh was different from most Nam in that he was an individual given to serious contemplation who allowed his mind to roam freely. Like original thinkers today who often assume that they are the only ones who have this capability, Namuh was unaware of others who might be thinking along the same lines. The restrictive nature of the Crew Elders further contributed to this isolation as most Nam were afraid to talk to others about new or innovative ideas.

Namuh thought about everything, *the meaning of his life, the welfare of the Nam people, and most of all, he wondered if there was any greater purpose for his life.* It was forbidden by the Law of the Log to think in this manner because it was an indication that one who did so considered himself special or unique. It was not that Namuh thought himself better than others or special. *He thought each Nam individual was special and that each could contribute much more to the whole of Nam if they could only know their special purpose and realize their own potential.*

He supposed that the inclination to think as he did came from his father who had been a friend of Renni Nam. Renni Nam, now banished as a "No Nam" from the Valley of the Nam, had been a revered teacher who had taught that *the power to transform the lives of the Nam was within themselves.* Namuh believed this to be true, but now Renni Nam was only a distant memory.

For reasons Namuh did not quite comprehend, the memory of Renni Nam figured strongly in his thinking. He could be working in the fields or sitting on the hillside in the evenings, and memories of his teachings would come back to him. It was like someone talking to him from the dim past.

Namuh had been a small boy at the time of the banishment, but he remembered the sage's visits to his home on the hillside. He remembered only vaguely Renni Nam's discourses to those who came to hear him and was too young to understand a great deal. He did remember that Renni Nam had talked of a God even more powerful than Pilot and he had called this God Efil. This talk had lead to a confrontation with the Crew Elders, and the charge of heresy by Raef, the Crew Elder second only to Worran.

Namuh realized that Renni Nam was on his mind a great deal, but he thought it was because he missed his father so much. It was as if when he thought of one or the other of the two most important individuals in his early life, both were brought to mind. Namuh's father had known Renni Nam from their childhood. Namuh remembered how frightened he was that the Crew Elders would come for his father when they banished Renni Nam as a "No Nam". They had been such close friends, but his father was only a farmer with no additional skills and had never been seen as a promoter of Renni Nam's teaching.

Namuh's father had said that Renni Nam was considered a little strange and was withdrawn from the other children when they were young. He was different from the other boys his age, but as they grew older, Renni Nam had become a teacher. He had earned the respect of both parents and students. Namuh's father had become more and more attracted to his teachings and had hoped his son would be a good student. Namuh knew that these teachings were different from the Law of the Log, but because Renni Nam was banished when Namuh was so young, and because of concern for what the Crew Elders might do, his father rarely mentioned him or spoke of his teachings.

Renni Nam had noticed Namuh and had told his father, "Even though Namuh is only a child, someday he will be a credit to the people of Nam." He had said, "Namuh's questions and quiet thoughtful manner mean that someday he will ask the kinds of questions that will lead many to look for answers. He reminds me of myself when I was a boy." When Renni Nam was banished, Namuh's father had been very upset but had said little. Though Namuh asked many questions, it was years later before he understood why the teachings of Renni Nam had caused the banishment.

Namuh's father had thought that Renni Nam's prediction meant that Namuh would grow up to be a teacher. Namuh, however, had seemed reserved and withdrawn. He even became prone to what his father took to be self-doubt and timidity. Certainly, Dimit, Namuh's best friend, was a timid sort of child, and Namuh spent a great deal of time with him. They spent a lot more time in the hills and the lower levels of the mountains than they did in serious study or work.

There were no schools now except the one run by the Crew Elders, and their training was primarily strong discipline in the

Law of the Log. Of course, agriculture and animal husbandry were taught, but this kind of training usually fell to the parents. There was training in such skills as carpentry and masonry, but these skills were learned as apprentices, and the Crew Elders looked upon these skills as a lower level of learning. The highest form of knowledge was the Law of the Log.

It had all been different when Renni Nam was in the valley. He had sought to expand the thinking of the Nam, to inspire his students to look for solutions to problems that faced the Nam people. He had stressed the power of the individual to effect change in themselves and the people of Nam as a whole. That was all in the past, however, and now no one spoke of Renni Nam. According to the Crew Elders, he had been seduced by Missile and blasphemed against the Great God Pilot.

Namuh grew up to be as hardworking as his father and a diligent student of the Law of the Log. However, he always had more questions than the Crew Elders knew the answers to, or were willing to answer. As he grew older, he retreated nightly to the hillside to be alone and to think. He loved to pose questions and think about the possible answers. He wanted answers more than anything else in the world. How he missed his father, and he missed the excitement of Renni Nam's visits.

After Renni Nam was gone, and as Namuh grew older, he had spent a great deal of time around the fires at night where the Crew Elders told their stories about Pilot. The Crew Elders were very good story-tellers and applied their skills to whatever concerned the Nam people at the time. There had been more excitement in the teachings of Renni Nam, such as he could remember, but the Crew Elders said that the ways of Missile, the evil one, were often more exciting. For one to dwell on Missile or anything but the Law of the Log could lead the unwary to destruction. Their stories of the fire that rained from the heavens when the Nam had dared disobey Pilot, and of what might happen if they did so again, were vivid.

Namuh was more than intrigued by the story of how Pilot had come and his actions while in the valley. He thought *there*

9

were great lessons to be learned from the Log, but wondered if there weren't a great deal more to them. Only Worran, the Navigator, head of the Crew Elders, kept the Log, and only the Crew Elders were taught by Worran. Namuh thought *the day might come when he would attain some recognition from Worran or the Crew Elders. He had hoped that he would be able to study from the Great Log. He had thought that it would have answers that could be found nowhere else.* As the years passed with no word on his request to enter the Council for study, he had ceased to harbor any hopes of this.

CHAPTER THREE

THE ORIGIN

The Log had been left, as legend told it, by the Great God Pilot, who had flown into the valley inside a Great Bird in the dim past. From the Great Bird's ear he had come forth, the creator of the valley and everything in it. All the Nam knew him as the fierce and mighty war god who could kill simply by pointing his hand. Thunder and lighting would explode from it, and the disobedient ones died instantly.

The Great God Pilot had abandoned them once. He had flown away in the Great Bird and had returned only after Nam Valley's greatest day of calamity and after the unceasing prayers of the Nam people. The evil one, Missile, had come upon them, and there had been lights in the sky. A searing noise like thousands of trumpets had sounded, and it had seemed as if the sky had rained fire.

The Nam who survived, their children and their children's children would carry in their hearts the horror of Missile and the destruction that awaited those who did not obey the Great God Pilot. He had said that it was the duty of the Nam to always remain diligent in their remembrances of Him. Had He not destroyed the children of Missile who had come upon the Valley of the Nam? If it had not been for Him, the Nam would have been wiped out to the last individual.

When he had departed, he had promised to come again and take everyone over the mountain ranges to a valley many times more wonderful than the Valley of the Nam. "There", he said, "the winters are not fierce and crops can be grown year around." It was the land of the gods, and the Nam would become like gods. He left behind his sacred book known as the Great Log.

Worran's ancestors had been the keepers of the Log, and the Crew Elders were dedicated to the Navigator.

Worran had revealed more about Pilot than his predecessors and thus was considered the greatest of the Navigators. It was Worran who revealed the words from Pilot himself, "I am the beginning and the end and you shall have no other gods but me." Pilot had said, "The Nam people originated with Me and you are my people." There was no question - Pilot was a jealous god.

Namuh had memorized the stories from the Great Log, as told by Worran and the Crew elders. He daily prayed to Pilot but thought that *He must have forgotten the Nam because they suffered much each year and without respite from the fierce winters He sent upon the valley. If he really cared anything about them, He wouldn't let this happen to them year after year.*

Namuh would never dare to say as much for fear he would be declared a "No Nam". He could imagine nothing worse. Renni Nam himself had said, "The Great God Pilot is real but he is not who and what Worran says he is." Renni Nam had been specific in his statement, "Pilot is not the Creator God". Renni Nam's banishment stemmed from this and other similar teachings.

Namuh never talked to anyone, even his family, about his own doubts concerning Pilot and his commitment to the Nam. Namuh was considered a simple, hard working man, who did his duty to the best of his ability and did not concern himself with higher matters. He was thought to be a bit of a dreamer. He spent as much time alone on the hillside as possible, often letting his mind dwell on Pilot, the legends and the needs of his fellow Nam. He had a contemplative nature and hid his thoughts wisely.

The lessons of the Crew Elders about the love of Pilot for the Nam simply did not seem to match the stories about his actions when He had come to the valley. They told of how some Nam had disobeyed Pilot and had been struck dead when he pointed his hand at them. Fear had been established in their hearts from the first moment Pilot had come.

The admonition, as taught by the Crew Elders, and supposedly coming from the Great Log, was to fear and obey Pilot. The command to love all the Nam was the second in importance, but few could get past the first law. When Pilot was mentioned, all Nam hearts froze with the terror of him.

Namuh mused on the fate of the people as he walked through fields of freshly planted Wonk. He had no doubts about the harvest as they were always bountiful; but he always had doubts about the winter. Winter was the one big concern in the life of the Nam people.

If they could collectively have asked Pilot for one thing, there was no doubt it would be to reduce the harshness of their winters. The concept of making the winters more manageable seemed to be beyond the understanding of the Nam. They had fire and skins from the animals that roamed the hills, but that was the extent of their adaptation to the weather.

For Namuh there was a second serious concern. *He was afraid of Raef and his wife, Regna. Raef would someday be the Navigator. He was the heir apparent to Worran, but unlike Worran, who inspired no fear in the hearts of the Nam, Raef was a foreboding presence. Namuh hoped it would never happen that Raef become the Navigator, but it seemed inevitable. Namuh thought that Raef must crave the power that would become his with the death of Worran who was elderly. The only thing that held him back was the power bestowed on Worran by the Law of the Log*. This was Namuh's observation, and he intuitively felt this. He did not know if anyone else had this view because he never talked about it with anyone.

Namuh knew Raef was dangerous, but his wife, Regna, some considered to be even more unpredictable. It was she who years ago had railed against Renni Nam, the Sage, until he was banished to the mountains as a "No Nam". She had wanted him killed, but Worran had ruled in favor of making him "No Nam" instead. In her rage, it was as if there was no rational thought at all. She literally got her way because everyone wanted to avoid conflict with her.

Her power was seeded in the fact that she was Raef's wife. She had no official position. Namuh thought *she was like a reflection of Raef's thoughts. Raef thought - Regna acted*. Etam, Namuh's wife, surprised him one day by saying what Namuh already secretly thought. "Even though Raef is a Crew Elder, he is the poison and Regna the visible result of it." This was not a subject Namuh was comfortable discussing, and he quickly changed the subject.

Privately he thought that *Etam was more observing than he had imagined, and that someday he would discuss the matters that constantly dwelled on his mind with her. She was probably the only one he could ever talk to about his worries. Until this point he had thought that he was the only one concerned about the future of the Nam.*

Namuh's father had said that he did not understand all that Renni Nam taught, but that he was a good man whose wisdom he used to the benefit of the Nam. He had been perceived a threat to the Crew Elders, but all of this was a long time ago and fuzzy in Namuh's memory. When the Nam began seeking out Renni Nam for his advice and council and listening to his discourses on almost any subject he chose to address, the Crew Elders complained that their position and authority were being undermined. No one was more vocal about the dangers of listening to Renni Nam than Regna.

Regardless of what the Crew Elders or even Worran said, Namuh knew *Renni Nam must have been a wise teacher. His ideas about building storage houses for Wonk and other preparations for winter had only been laughed at by the Crew Elders. What had sent Regna into a fit of rage was Renni Nam's talk of a God infinitely more powerful than Pilot. Worst of all was Renni Nam's assertion that this powerful God could live inside each of the Nam*. He had called this God, Efil, whom he said was the force of all life.

Renni Nam had been banished years ago, and many thought him dead. Who could live in the mountains above and without Wonk, especially with the harsh winters? But Namuh thought that *some evenings on the hillside, Renni Nam was close. He thought he had seen his fire in the mountains and believed he had seen him just above his hillside on a jutting rock, standing straight and tall, silhouetted by the moon. Namuh thought he might have been dreaming and could not be sure.* On this occasion, he had quietly talked about what he had seen with Etam, but she had said nothing.

CHAPTER FOUR

THE LAW OF THE LOG

A strict code had been left in the Great Log. The Law of the Log was clear, and those who disobeyed were either put to death or declared "No Nam". By the age of Nam adulthood, all could recite the Twelve Commandments of the Law of the Log by heart. The Crew Elders interpreted the Laws for the Nam because the meaning of the Great Log had been revealed only to them. All the Crew Elders were descendants of early Nam who had been present when Pilot had come in the Great Bird.

The Crew Elders said that the Great God Pilot was a God of love. Renni Nam had said he was a "War God", not that the people of Nam knew what war really meant. The Nam had never known war. In their language there was no word for war. It was something that only Pilot and Missile did. Renni Nam had taught that war meant "One who rules by force."

The Nam did not know where the legend about the war of the gods had come from. The Crew Elders no longer acknowledged that there had been any such war. In any event, the gist of the legend was that Missile and the Great God Pilot had fought against one another for some reason. They had tried to kill each other, but no one knew why this might have been, nor how such a thing could have happened.

It was true Pilot was not to be questioned and that his punishment could be swift and deadly. When Pilot first came to the valley, many Nam did not obey him at first and were killed instantly as he called down thunder through his hand.

Worran had revealed many of the secrets to some of the Crew Elders. These were secrets no previous Navigator had revealed about the coming of the Great God Pilot. These Crew Elders had, in turn, revealed a great deal to others before Worran

16

could silence them. He had not meant to feed speculation but he knew this to be more than a legend. The reason Pilot had come to the Valley of the Nam had indeed been because of a war between the gods.

No one but the Crew Elders were allowed to see the Log, so the Nam were familiar only with the laws as revealed by the Crew Elders in their wisdom, and at their discretion. The laws were recited each year at the Harvest Festival, and there was no mistaking their meaning.

The language of the gods had been given to the ancient prophets of Nam and the Law of the Log had been translated into the Nam language by the ancestors of Worran. Only they had known what the Laws meant. Worran was never as certain of these translations as he professed to be with his students and the Crew Elders. He had been taught the ancient language of the gods by his father. He knew what was written, but how his forefathers had come to the exact wording in the language of the Nam, he had been told, was with the assistance of the Great God Pilot Himself.

One with the perspective of modern man would look at the Laws of the Log with different eyes than the Nam. Their perspective might be compared to the ancient Hebrew prophet in the biblical text who reported viewing a fiery chariot, which came down from the sky to pick up Elijah the Prophet. This was the only way the prophet could have described it. He had no other point of reference. The Nam also could view the events of their history only from their perspective.

The original text in the Captain's Log, which the Nam people as a whole were never allowed to see, is provided for the reader. The Law of the Log as Namuh and the Nam people received it from the Crew Elders is shown in capital letters. The thoughts of Namuh concerning these laws are recorded in italics.

1) (The Original Text) "The Pilot is Commander of this mission, and his decisions must be respected and obeyed. Your Navigator is second in command. It is

17

essential that at no time any sign of disrespect for your officers be shown. The people will be watching and take notice of your behavior."

(The Crew Elders' Translation) ALL NAM ARE TO LOVE AND OBEY PILOT.

(Namuh thought) *Pilot can demand and command the respect of the Nam because of his power and make the Nam fear him,* but he wondered, *How can he command love? Love may be earned, but how do you force anyone to love?*

2) (The Original Text) "The Crew must function as one, a team, respect the skills of each other and work together for the successful fulfillment of the mission. There must be no dissension among the crew as you must command the respect of the people."

(The Crew Elders' Translation) ALL NAM ARE TO LOVE EACH OTHER AS PART OF THE WHOLE. ALL NAM ARE OF A COMMON BOND AND EXIST ONLY AS A PART OF THE WHOLE COMMUNITY. NAM EXIST FOR EACH OTHER AND NOT FOR THEMSELVES.

(Namuh thought*) I understand how each Nam is part of the whole of the Nam community, but why do they put such emphasis on our mission or purpose if the individual entity has no importance?*

3) (The Original Text) "The Crew must at all cost complete this mission. The people of this valley must be controlled by martial law if necessary. They must become supportive of your mission, and you must see to their welfare. Pacification of the inhabitants is necessary."

(The Crew Elders' Translation) ALL OF THE NAM HAVE A FUNCTION TO FULFILL IN LIFE, AND THIS FUNCTION IS THEIR "MISSION". ONLY THE CREW ELDERS ARE TO DETERMINE WHAT EACH NAM SHOULD BE AND DO WITH HIS LIFE.

(Namuh thought) *This law disallows the self-determination of each individual Nam. How can the proper merit of a Nam be determined if based upon total unequivocal obedience or blind faith in the Crew Elders?*

4) (The Original Text) "The Navigator shall determine the flight plan and is alone responsible for decoding said course. The Crew must convince the population of the danger they face of invasion by the enemy."

(The Crew Elders' Translation) THE LAW IS THE FINAL JUDGE IN THE NAM'S LIFE AND THE CREW ELDERS ONLY SHALL DETERMINE THE MEANING OF THE LAWS. ANY CONTRAVENTION OF THE LAW WILL BRING SWIFT PUNISHMENT. PILOT WILL RELEASE MISSILE FROM HIS PRISON, AND MISSILE WILL RAIN FIRE ON THE NAM.

(Namuh thought) *There are Crew Elders who have shown great wisdom, but many are just like the rest of us. They have ambitions and appear to be more interested in power than ministering to the people of Nam. How can I fully trust the decisions of the Crew Elders?*

5) (The Original Text) "This mission is of vital importance to the nation, as well as the individual interest of Crew members and the population of the valley must be subservient."

(The Crew Elders' Translation) NO NAM HAS A RIGHT TO EXIST OTHER THAN AS A PART OF THE WHOLE NAM COMMUNITY. THE NAM'S HIGHEST ALLEGIANCE IS TO THE NAM COMMUNITY AND THE GREAT GOD PILOT.

(Namuh thought*) This appears to be a repetition of the second law. Why the emphasis on the lack of importance of the individual? What are they afraid the individual Nam might do?*

6) (The Original Text) "This mission may call for sacrifice in the face of adverse circumstances. This is a team effort. You are a unit working as one and the people of the valley must be molded into a support unit totally dedicated to you. All the provisions you require must come from this valley, and it must remain your base until further notice."

(The Crew Elders' Translation) ALL NAM THOUGHT SHALL BE DIRECTED TOWARD THE COMMON GOOD, AND THE SACRIFICE OF ONE NAM FOR ANOTHER IS THE HIGHEST POSSIBLE ASPIRATION. ALL NAM THOUGHT IS INSIGNIFICANT WHEN NOT PART OF THE COMMON OBJECTIVE.

(Namuh thought*) If the thinking of the Nam individual is unimportant and insignificant, why are they afraid of independent thought?*

7) (The Original Text) "Your individual missions must be clearly understood by all in the event of a loss of a Crew member. The people of the valley must be organized for maximum production."

(The Crew Elders' Translation) NO NAM INDIVIDUAL IS OTHER THAN WHAT HE APPEARS TO BE, AND NO NAM IS DIFFERENT FROM ANOTHER NOR MAY HE HAVE ANY PART OF HIMSELF THAT IS NOT TO BE KNOWN BY ALL OTHER NAM.

(Namuh thought*) I have many thoughts that I cannot reveal, and possibly others too have such thoughts. How can a law control my inner thoughts? What harm can our individual thinking cause the people of Nam? Maybe if the individual thoughts of the Nam were known, answers could be found to our worst problems.*

8) (The Original Text) "The Crew must work as a finely tuned unit with maximum cooperation, using your best judgment and with the benefit of your respective specialties. Make suggestions and share ideas. Establish intelligence units among the people. No resistance or underground can be allowed to develop."

(The Crew Elders' Translation) NO NAM MAY POSSESS ANY KNOWLEDGE OTHER THAN WHAT HAS BEEN REVEALED IN THE GREAT LAW OF THE LOG. SHOULD A NAM CONCEIVE OF AN IDEA NOT ALREADY KNOWN AND TAUGHT BY THE CREW ELDERS, IT IS HIS DUTY TO REVEAL THE THOUGHT TO THE CREW ELDERS FOR DISCUSSION.

(Namuh thought) *They must be afraid of knowledge in the hands of the Nam people. I have no problem with sharing my thoughts, but it is obviously dangerous to do so. Look what happened to Renni Nam. How can any authority, even Pilot, enforce such a law?*

9) (The Original Text) "All of you have volunteered for this mission, and it is expected that you will give your

all. As far as possible, form a consensus, mobilize your resources and execute the plan of action on the ground."

(The Crew Elders' Translation) NAM ARE TO GIVE OF THEIR WEALTH ONLY FOR THE COMMON GOOD, AND ONLY THE CREW ELDERS SHALL DECIDE WHAT THE COMMON GOOD IS.

(Namuh thought*) A government or authority can force me to part with the product of my labor. They are the power, but if they were a responsible power, they could solve our problems. The Crew Elders do not seem to want to address our severest problems. Why?*

10) (The Original Text) "Your nation's vital interest is at stake, and the interest of the nation is your primary objective."

(The Crew Elders' Translation) ALL NAM ARE TO RESPECT THE NAM RACE AND PILOT, THE GOD OF THE NAM. THEY MUST ASPIRE TO NO GREATER OBJECTIVE THAN THE LAW OF THE LOG WHICH IS THE PATH TO NAM SALVATION.

(Namuh thought*) I have always shown respect for Pilot and my own kind. The Nam people and their welfare are foremost on my mind, but what greater objective might there be? Is there something else that has not been revealed to us?*

11) (The Original Text) "No secondary objective shall be contemplated due to the importance of your primary mission. If you vary from the flight plan, your craft may be destroyed by friendly fire. No promises can be given to the people of the valley with regard to immediate removal from danger. Their manpower will be required.

These people are primitive and cannot be allowed to expect assistance in the short term."

(The Crew Elders' Translation) THE NAM PEOPLE SHALL NOT EXPECT MORE THAN THE LIMITATIONS PLACED ON THEM BY THEIR ENVIRONMENT AND THE WILL OF THE GREAT GOD PILOT. NAM CANNOT HAVE EVERYTHING THEY WANT. TO DESIRE MORE IS A CONTRAVENTION OF THE LAW.

(Namuh thought) *What could we expect to do but improve on what we have? Are we not to aspire to such things as breaking the cycle of winter starvation? Why can we not desire something better? What would happen if all the Nam voiced their desires?*

What could be clearer? The laws were severe, but they were the laws and must be obeyed to the letter. The Nam understood these laws because of the expert translations of the Crew Elders, their insightful discourses and the infallibility of the Navigator, Worran, who presided over the Crew Elders. Aside from the Great God Pilot himself, the Navigator was the highest rank. His was a unique position in the Valley of the Nam.

CHAPTER FIVE

WORRAN

There was continuous debate among the Crew Elders on all matters concerning the Law of the Log. This was considered study and discourse of the highest kind. It was from these debates that great speeches had been delivered and printed for the people of Nam. Some of these speeches were considered masterpieces. In matters of great import, they were used to establish the law of the land. They were quoted and discussed in great detail becoming a part of the Nam tradition as if they were part of the Log. They were the words of the greatest thinkers and their interpretations of the law.

Because of their personal instruction by Worran in the Law of the Log and their many years of training, the priests had the sum total of Nam knowledge at their disposal. The base of the religion of the Nam was simple obedience of the law or whatever the Crew Elders determined to be the meaning of the law. One either adhered to the teachings of the Great Log or one was declared a "No Nam".

The more dangerous transgressors were put to death, a drastic step unheard of before the coming of Pilot and alien to the nature of the Nam people. Such punishment had still been rare until the rise to prominence in the Council of Raef. The more common punishment had been banishment, and this too had not been common until Raef. Aside from death by stoning, being branded a "No Nam" was the most feared sentence in the valley.

Before the coming of Pilot, the King and Queen had been leaders. Each Nam had been responsible for himself. Each was a sovereign person who nominated his leaders based upon their knowledge and their ability to lead. It was with the advent of

Pilot that fear and the concept of war had been introduced. The Nam had not known fear nor had war ever been a plague upon their society. They had worked together because it was to the benefit of each to do so. Individually, the understanding of their responsibility for their own actions had led them to cooperate with each other.

The Nam individual had never been subservient to the whole of the Nam body, a state or any one group. They understood the principles of Efil, which was their God of Life, but Pilot had replaced Efil primarily because of the creation of the priest cast. Because of the power he had displayed, Pilot had shown himself to be the superior god in their minds.

The Crew Elders were the guardians of the Log and Pilot's representatives. They had shown the Nam people how ignorant they had been to depend on such superstitions! Pilot had been a real presence they could see and hear. They had witnessed his power to kill, and he had promised salvation someday. He would take them to the valley without winters. There in the home of the gods, they could escape the harsh winters and life would be easy.

Worran was considered the wisest among the Nam. It was said that his ancestors had talked personally with Pilot. He alone had seen the Great Log in its entirety, with its many sacred symbols and images. The Law of the Log had been revealed to Worran by his father. His grandfather had revealed it to his father before him. Now, Worran was the last in the line. He had never married and had no son to whom the title of Navigator could be passed. There would be a new line of Navigators beginning with Raef.

Only on the rare occasions when Worran had no choice but to speak, concerning matters of some importance to the people of Nam, did he muster the courage to do so. It was not so much that he was afraid to speak in public. He simply had great feelings of inadequacy. It was his limited ability to think outside the boundaries of the law, which left him ill at ease.

25

Because he spoke so seldom, he was thought to be very wise. Deep down, Worran had never believed himself worthy of the position of Navigator and knew it was simply a matter of being the son of a Navigator that gave him the privileges he enjoyed.

Worran had only the Law of the Log to cling to. In a land of limited intuitive thought, Worran knew his limitations, but his role as Navigator gave him no latitude to learn. He was expected to know and to teach. He could never reveal his feelings of inadequacy nor ever appear uncertain. He was the representative of Pilot, and this great responsibility rested heavily upon his shoulders.

In his own way, Worran was a most impressive man, and the wisdom of the Log was the seat of his power. The remarkable thing about Worran was that he never seemed to do anything. He did not, in any way, initiate action. He would listen to the Crew Elders argue some proposed action or punishment and then sleep on it. These nights were a torture to him because making decisions of import were very difficult for him.

Worran relied on a strict interpretation of the law to see him through difficult times. In the end, he would make the final decision or render his verdict in an authoritarian manner as if it had been a personal revelation from the Great God Pilot. He had no particular goals or agenda for the Crew Elders as planning was not his strong suit. He held no great vision for the people of Nam.

There was no civilian administration or government outside of the King and Queen. They could often be seen among the people but exercised no power. They were loved and revered by the Nam much as the Monarchy in some countries today. However, there were no non-religious leaders or administrators. Worran alone was all-powerful because the Law of the Log had so designated.

From time to time, he held council with Queen Yhtapa. It was infrequent, however, that he would meet with King Tnetopmi. Worran simply had no time for the King. If it had not been for Yatapa, Worran would have done away with the monarchy a long time ago.

Tnetopmi's court was open to the people, but he functioned only as an ear. Much was made over the King and Queen at the Festival of the Harvest as this was the major event of the year. Yhtapa was revered in the valley but not because she did anything for the people. She wielded no power but was like a mother to them. You might say she gave them a warm feeling but little else.

People in need would solicit Worran's help through Yhtapa, and she was credited with the results when it was favorable. While she and the King talked with Worran, it was only a courtesy extended by him. If anyone did have influence with Worran, it was Yhtapa because her presence seemed to reflect the people of Nam. Worran loved her sunny disposition and enjoyed her company. If there was a matter that truly concerned her, he would try to do what he could. Worran also knew that only Yhtapa had any place in the heart of the Nam people.

If King Tnetopmi had any power or ever exercised any power, none of the Nam had seen him do so. It was as if he was there only to complement the Queen. Yhtapa, it was said, expressed the desires of the Nam to Worran, but only Worran knew whether he actually responded to any of their desires. Since Yhtapa told Worran what the King wanted, no one really knew if it was what they both wanted, what Tnetopmi wanted or what Yhtapa wanted.

This was a working cooperation, with the Crew Elders supporting the King and Queen and the King and Queen supporting the Crew elders.

The government of the Valley of Nam was a theocracy, a nation ruled by religious law. Crew Elders were the only interpreters of the law. The Law of the Log had been sufficient for their fathers, and, as far a Worran was concerned, it was sufficient for the Nam today. The Law of the Log was the direct revelation of the Great God Pilot, and Worran was duty bound to fulfill his will and uphold the traditions based on the Log.

27

CHAPTER SIX

THE MISSION

In the quiet of the evening, high on the hillside, Namuh contemplated the stars, saying aloud to the wind, "There must be an answer to this never ending cycle of plenty and starvation; this "nose to the grind" existence we lead, with survival the sole objective." Of course he knew none could hear him. Sometimes he wished he could again talk to his father, or maybe even to Renni Nam in the mountains, but that was ridiculous. His father was dead now, and Renni Nam, banished as a "No Nam" was probably dead as well. Whether God was called Pilot or Efil mattered little to him but *he wanted to understand his own purpose.*

He was not satisfied with the declaration of the Crew Elders that his mission was to work in the fields and dedicate his life to feeding the Nam people. There was nothing wrong with this mission, but he did not see the production of Wonk and Feileb as a very difficult task. The valley produced far more Wonk than could be consumed even in the harshest winters. *The problem was wastage and the resulting times of great need.*

Namuh had many questions and sincerely sought the answers in the only way he knew how. Renni Nam was gone, the Crew Elders had no answers and the questions in his mind seemed to multiply faster than he could reason out the old ones. *He wanted to understand who he was and who the Nam people were. He knew most Nam would not even think along these lines, and that the Crew Elders, if they knew, were not inclined to address the subject. He wondered about the stories of Pilot and how he had killed those who did not obey him. It seemed so at odds with the teachings about the God of love. Then there was the threat that Pilot would allow Missile to destroy all the*

28

Nam that had not been faithful to the Law of the Log.   This idea disturbed him most.

Why had Pilot chosen the Nam as his special people? What did this mean anyway?   Were there others, and what were they like?   Were they already in the valley with no winters?   Did Pilot live with them or in still another valley?   If there were other valleys as they were told, and someday Pilot would take them to such a valley, why were the good people like Renni Nam allowed to suffer banishment when those like Raef were allowed to flourish in places of prominence?   Is there really such a thing as justice?   Is the world one of order or random chaos?   Who is responsible, if anyone, for anything that happens?   And there was much more that Namuh wanted to know.

He knew he could not ask these questions, but he wondered, *"Why were only the Crew Elders allowed to see the secret Law of the Log?   What if their interpretation was wrong?   What if Renni Nam was right, and Pilot was not the real God? Assuming he existed, what if he were just a powerful being from one of the other valleys?"*   He knew this was the kind of thinking that had caused the banishment of Renni Nam and that he dare not discuss the matter with anyone, but neither could he put the questions out of his mind.

One night as Namuh leaned back against a small tree on the hillside, he began to doze off to sleep.   It had been a hard day in the fields. He had worked mechanically with his hands doing the work, but his mind was on his questions.   Presently he felt himself to be very light and floating.   Looking down, he could see himself sleeping against the tree.   He felt as if he was being drawn up toward the stars.   A being, whose light was so bright that he could not directly look at him, appeared.   He felt warm in the light of this being's presence but still could not see him.

The light of the being adjusted, and it was as if two ordinary people had sat down to talk together.   *So this is Pilot*, he thought. He did not seem the fearsome God of the Nam with the sacred name, Pilot.   He seemed concerned for the welfare of the Nam and talked with Namuh as a friend might. They discussed what was on Namuh's mind as if they were old acquaintances; as if they had known each other a long time. He took Namuh up so that he could see over the mountain ranges to other valleys, and there was no Great Bird to carry them. There had been the sensation of heights and movement - then they were there.

He showed Namuh the beautiful valleys far over the mountain ranges surrounding the Valley of the Nam. He showed him the passes through the mountains. One of the passes was a tunnel through a mountain, and it opened behind a hut. He had never seen a hut that close to a mountain. This meant that there was someone who knew about the tunnel but had told no one. Instead of what had appeared the most accessible routes, the ones that the Nam had tried, the most available pass was through the great mountain nearest his own beloved hillside.

He was told not to worry about Raef and Regna. He was assured that they could not harm Namuh or the people of Nam unless they themselves allowed it to happen. The power to stop them was theirs. He said they did not and would not have any power over the people of Nam if the people knew the truth.

He also offered a solution for the harshness of Nam life. God said, "Build a house according to the specifications I will give you, and you will always have Wonk in abundance. The cycle of winter hardship will be broken. This I promise. In this house you will find the Laws that govern the universe, and these truths will make you free."

When Namuh awoke, he was again in his body under the tree. He frantically sought a way to remember all of the instructions he had received. What did Pilot say? Yes, He said there was a pass through the great mountain nearest his hillside, but escape was not the answer. He said Raef and Regna would lose their positions of power. He also said, "Build Me a House." Build a house for God! *What a job! What an honor to be chosen to build a house for God!*

What else? Yes, He said that He would reveal the Universal Laws in His house! These Laws, God had said, would reveal His very being because they were part of his "Divine Expression." "The Laws will make you free", He had said. Free from what? Namuh could only wonder. *He supposed it meant that the Nam would be free from the cycle of winter hardship*!

Well, Namuh thought, *I think I know what God has said and what he wants me to do, but I forgot to ask him whether his Name was Pilot or Efil. It was all too fantastic for words. The vision had been so real as if he were really there. The way his body felt, the lightness, the way they moved and what he had beheld with his own eyes. He had never had a dream like this and was unsure and shaken by the experience, but he knew one thing above all else - he must build this house for God.*

The plan for construction, if not the intent of God's words, was crystal clear in Namuh's mind. He was to build the house of a most peculiar design, unlike any other structure in the valley. It was to be an upright cylinder jutting into the sky more than three times as high as any in the valley. No one had a house more than two floors. Even the palace of Tnetopmi and Yhtapa was only three floors high.

The house Namuh was to build had to be reinforced at several points making three main divisions with a total of seven levels. There was to be a shaft running from the ground to the roof with a pulley system for moving offerings, Namuh supposed, which would be brought by the people for God. In the roof there was to be an opening, again he supposed *this would allow God to come and go; or maybe this is how He will bring the Wonk to us*, He thought.

Namuh was shocked by the clarity of what he thought must have been a dream, yet *it must have been God. Who else would want a house with so many floors and such a strange design? None of the Nam needed such a house as this*. Namuh could not even have imagined such a house, so the idea had to have been from God. If only he could talk with his father or Renni Nam. They would know what it all meant.

Nam had inhabited the valley for thousands of years, and no Nam had built such a house or even imagined a structure like the

31

one described by Pilot. No Nam knew of a pass or had even suspected that one existed in the great mountain closest to the valley. No Nam could promise the banishment of Raef and Regna or even imagine that they could be controlled. No Nam could promise that there would always be enough Wonk regardless of the weather. Despite his doubts, Namuh wanted to set out immediately to build the house for God, but first he had to reveal his communication with Pilot to the Crew Elders. This was the law.

CHAPTER SEVEN

MISSION ACCEPTED

Namuh requested an audience with the Crew Elders. First he addressed the august Council in the time-honored way saying, "May the Council Members and the Navigator have Mod in abundance always." He then explained as best he could what had happened, describing the events of the previous evening with as much detail as possible.

To his surprise, the Crew Elders appeared agitated. They were not just puzzled or questioning, like Namuh. They were angry. Raef brooded at Namuh's revelation, his face a dark portrait of hatred. Namuh wondered *why Raef should hate him as he was only following the law and revealing what had happened. Namuh thought that if Regna had been in the Council Chamber there would have been violence.*

Even Worran, the Navigator himself, spoke disparagingly of Namuh's experience. His normally melodious voice was strained as if he could barely suppress some inner fear or anger. Worran said, "If it were really Pilot, why had He not talked to his Navigator and representative to the people of Nam?" To himself, he wondered if Namuh might not be the new messenger of Pilot. Maybe Pilot was displeased with his Navigator in some way. But he said, "Pilot would not have chosen to reveal his plan to one who is not even a Crew Elder."

"And what of this nonsense about Universal Laws being revealed in the house?" Raef asked "If Pilot was going to come to this house and reveal new laws, why would he not have told the Navigator to build it?" Some Crew Elders said, "This simply cannot be true. This has to be the fantasy of an idle mind."

It was the opinion of many Crew Elders that Namuh spent too much time on the hillsides and not enough on his duties.

Still others said, "You must have been listening to the ranting of Renni Nam." They asked him if he had been in the mountains and seen Renni Nam. Namuh was so frightened by the response and the questions about Renni Nam that he did not even remind them that Renni Nam was supposed to be dead.

It wasn't until later that it occurred to Namuh that the Crew Elders must think Renni Nam is alive. The reprimand in their voices had made Namuh shrink in fear. He was not accustomed to talking to Crew Elders, much less Worran himself. He was so surprised by the reaction, he could hardly speak. *If this was to be the reaction of the Crew Elders, why had God come to him in the first place? Why had he told him to build Him a house?* It was all very confusing to Namuh.

Namuh was relieved of all duties and told to return to his home while the Council sat in session. He was not to work in the fields and was to talk to no one including his friends. Namuh wondered what he would say to his friend, Dimit. They had grown up together, and while he did not share his inner thoughts with Dimit, there was not a day passed that he did not spend time with him. He would have to discuss the matter with Etam because it directly affected the household. Besides, Etam would probably be the wisest counsel. She had amazed him with her insight before when he had thought no one else shared his concerns.

Dimit was a different matter. From an early age, he had been Namuh's closest friend. He was like a shadow, a quiet presence and always a little fearful when the subject of Pilot came up. Sometimes Namuh thought Dimit was wise in his ways, but how would he ever understand that what had happened to Namuh seemed now to have been real and not a dream?

Dimit would stand behind him, but Namuh had no doubt that it would be well behind him. Dimit would stand up to no one. He would always do as he was told. Anything but what the Crew Elders said, frightened him. In fact, even the lessons by the Crew Elders left him fretful and worried - especially those lessons conducted by Raef. He was afraid that if the Great God

Pilot came back, it would be to punish them, not to take them out of the valley. To Dimit, Missile was a nightmare waiting to happen.

Dimit was good-hearted and would never intentionally hurt anyone. It wasn't that he was physically afraid of anyone. It was more a matter of aversion to any kind of confrontation, even to the point that he would often give in to the desires of others when he was clearly right. Namuh knew that Dimit simply felt that there was nothing so important that it was necessary for him to assert his wishes.

Namuh could not tell Dimit about the dream or visitation because Worran had told him to tell no one what he had experienced. Dimit would have worried and no doubt would have suggested that Namuh go back to the Crew Elders and tell them it was all a mistake. He would want to be supportive, but Namuh did not want to cause his friend problems. **Even if he told him, and even if Dimit believed him, what could he do?** *What could he say to his family? He could be killed, or almost as bad, he could be declared a "No Nam" and banished, like Renni Nam, to the mountains. This was tantamount to a death sentence anyway.*

It was a fearful and dejected Namuh who returned home from the Council Meeting. He quietly went about his chores and waited until the evening meal to reveal the predicament in which he found himself.

Meanwhile, the Crew Elders had remained in Council long after Namuh had been sent away. There was much consternation, threats of punishment and worry about how this might affect the Nam people. Raef called for the death of Namuh before his evil and blasphemous story could be told to the Nam. "All liars shall have their place in the fire and devastation of Missile," Raef quoted from the Log. It was his favorite quotation.

However, as usual, Worran wanted to deliberate. In his mind, there was more to this whole matter, and he would have to be very careful. He would have the final word, and this was another of those burdens of leadership that weighed heavily upon him.   He felt his age today.   He said, "I will take this matter under consideration, and we will again meet to discuss the fate of Namuh in three days. In the meantime, Namuh is to speak to no one, and a guard will be placed at his home to ensure this."

CHAPTER EIGHT

THE SEARCH FOR RENNI NAM

When they had finished eating, Namuh gathered his family about him. Etam, his wife, had been busy with the evening meal when Hturt (pronounced Ha-Turt), their son, had come to tell her that one of the guards for the Crew Elders was at the gate but appeared to want nothing. Hturt told them that the guard had said, "I am doing my duty, and no one is to come or go from the house."

Ynomrah, Namuh's daughter, was frightened by the appearance of the guard, but Namuh said nothing and went straight to his chores. After the long, quiet supper, they were anxious to know what had happened at the Council Meeting.

Namuh told them of the day's events and that he was now under house arrest. "My fate", he said, "is in the hands of the Council and Worran." He told them in greater detail of his dream and the promises Pilot had made. He had not only said that Raef and Regna would be banished or lose their power, but that if he built the house as demanded, they would be free of the cycle of suffering brought on by the harsh winters.

"The Crew Elders are angry and anything could happen." He said, "I do not know what to do. The dream was very real, but I am afraid. It never occurred to me that Pilot would tell me to do something that the Crew Elders would not like. They are his representatives in the Valley of Nam. Now I am in trouble with them, and if I do not do what He said to do, I will be in trouble with Him."

Hturt said, "If Pilot is with you, how can the Crew Elders stand against his wishes?" Namuh said, "That is the point. They do not believe that He has told me anything. Even I, in the face of their anger, doubted whether or not it was Pilot.

Now I am in trouble and cannot discuss it even with my friends. You are my only counsel, and I must make a decision as to what to do. I suppose that the House Arrest applies to you as well. I guess I will just have to await their decision, which Worran will give in three days."

That night, as Namuh tossed restlessly in bed, Etam asked him what he intended to do. "You cannot just wait," she declared. Namuh cried out loud, "I know of nothing I can do but wait. I will again be allowed to relate the story of my encounter with Pilot. Then Worran and the Council of the Crew Elders will deliberate with Worran announcing the will of Pilot."

Worran had said, "This is not a matter that concerns anyone else." In other words, this would be a closed hearing because he wanted the Nam to know as little of what Namuh had to say about his visitation or dream as possible. He had decreed that no witnesses would be necessary. "This is a matter for the Great God Pilot to decide. Either Namuh is lying or he is not." None of Namuh's friends would be allowed to speak on his behalf, and he could not even relate to them what had happened.

Namuh said, "I doubt that anyone would believe me even if I could tell them." Etam lay quietly for a long time before again speaking. She spoke slowly but without hesitation. "There is but one thing to do. You must leave now, tonight, and go to the mountains. You must find Renni Nam and seek his counsel. No one else will know what you should do. You say that you think you have seen him, silhouetted by the moon as he looked from a ledge upon the valley. You have, on occasion, seen strange lights and have speculated upon whether or not he is alive. Go find him. If he cannot help you, stay with him or if you cannot find him, search for a means to survive in the mountains. If he has survived as you think he may have, so can you. It will be better to live there as a hermit and an outcast than to risk the penalty of death."

Namuh thought about this for so long, Etam thought he had gone to sleep. *Renni Nam, if he was alive, and if he could find him, would know what it all meant. He would know what to*

38

do. The worst that could happen would be that he would be unable to find him, in which case, he might freeze or starve to death. He might have to face death in numerous ways including the fierce lions that roamed the mountains. Even this would be better than being stoned to death or the humiliation and shame that would be brought upon him as a "No Nam". Etam was right. What choice did he have? He would go to the mountains and find Renni Nam or maybe Pilot would again come to him and tell him what to do.

He said nothing but rose and put on his warmest clothing. He embraced Etam. "You are a wise woman, and no Nam has had a better wife", he said. He then went to his sleeping children and kissed them for what he thought might be the last time and left their home with foreboding. The guard was at the gate, so he left by the back door and disappeared into the hills.

Where would he go? How would he find Renni Nam? He was not a hunter and didn't even have a weapon. How could he defend himself if he did come upon a wild animal? It had sounded like a good idea when Etam had suggested it, but facing the dark and looming mountains, he was not as sure as he had been. No one knew for sure Renni Nam was alive. Most thought him dead. He recalled what the Crew Elders had said about his talking to Renni Nam. *They think he may still be alive, and he may very well be out there somewhere*, but could he find him?

Namuh could only go into the mountains from the hillside in the direction from which he had seen the lights. If it was a fire it would have to have been at the edge of a cave because the wall of the mountain was shear, vertical rock. It had been a long time ago when he had seen the light, and could not be sure it had been a fire. *Maybe it was moonlight reflecting off some mirror-like rock. Where he thought that he had seen a form silhouetted in the moon was in the most impossible area. It had been straight up that big, old mountain behind his home and everyone knew there was no path.*

It was as if Namuh walked within himself. He paid no attention to where he went but climbed steadily past the hillside where God had come to him in the dream. He went further than he had ever been until the path became steep with only gnarled and stunted trees among the rocks. Long into the early morning hours, he climbed. In spite of the exertion of the climb, he grew colder. Then, there was no path, but still he climbed. He shivered with the cold even though he wore his heaviest and warmest coat. There seemed to be no end to the climb. Finally exhausted, he sat down on a ledge and looked out upon the valley.

Why had he ever revealed the dream to the Crew Elders? He knew if it had been Dimit, he would have said nothing. Dimit might be considered a fearful man by everyone who knew him, but would it not have been the wise way? But the question still loomed as a major factor, *What would he have said to Pilot if He had come again and asked why Namuh was not doing what He had told him to do? What could he have said to Him?*

If he was right in doing what he was doing, was he right about Renni Nam being alive? Even if he was right, he could not be sure of finding Renni Nam. If he found him alive, he could not be sure that Renni Nam could help him. What could Renni Nam do anyway? He was now a "No Nam". He would be satisfied, he thought, if Renni Nam could just tell him what it all meant. *Why would he have such a dream if it were not initiated by God? Why would He put him in such peril? The Crew Elders said that Pilot loved the Nam.*

He did not sleep that night and again began to climb with the first light. He could not look back and could hardly believe he had come to this point on the rock wall. He forged ahead, picking his way up the face of the peak in a sort of desperation effort and with little hope of finding anything but a crevice in which he could go no further. The other possibility was to find himself face to face with a mountain lion but neither thought caused him to hesitate. He climbed steadily.

In the distance, he could see bits of foliage stretching horizontally on the side of the mountain far above him. Maybe there was a ledge where he could rest. When he reached what he thought was the ledge, he found to his surprise that it was a small valley set back into the mountain that was not visible from below. The valley was so far up on the face of the peak that no one could have suspected its existence. Those who had gone looking for a pass had not tackled a direct assault on the old mountain nearest the valley but had gone the easier route through the distant but lower peaks.

It was not unlike the Valley of the Nam but much smaller. As he explored the valley, he found it to have trees though smaller than below in the valley. It was not so large that he could not explore it all within a short period of time. He was suddenly excited. There was a cultivated field hardly larger than the ample gardens that could be found near all the homes in the valley of the Nam, but there was an abundance of both Wonk and Feileb.

Nestled against the inner portion of the valley was a hut. Smoke curled upward from the thatched roof. Could this be any other than the home of Renni Nam? Who else could be living up here? He must have survived, and Namuh had been led straight to the Sage.

CHAPTER NINE

THE REVELATIONS OF RENNI NAM

Namuh knocked softly on the door, and it was immediately opened. There he stood. He was tall and erect in bearing, with a shock of white hair that looked as if it had never been groomed. Namuh knew it was the now infamous Renni Nam, though he had been so young when the sage had come to their home. What surprised Namuh most were the first words from the old Sage's mouth.

He did not begin with the traditional greeting. It was as if to Renni Nam, words about a house full of Mod, had no real meaning. He asked, "Are you the one who often comes to the hills in the night?" Namuh acknowledged that he was the one, and Renni Nam said, "I thought so. You come from the house near the hills that a friend of mine used to live in." Namuh said, "I have lived in this house from birth." Renni Nam smiled saying, "Then you can be none other than Namuh, my friend's son. How is your father?" Namuh said, "My father died 2 years ago, but he spoke of you often and even in his last days."

Renni Nam said, "Come in and warm yourself by the fire. Tell me why you have made this dangerous climb to see an old man who is an outcast from the Nam." Namuh warmed himself and sat down heavily for he was very tired. He asked, "Do you sometimes come down the mountain to the lower ledges? On one occasion I thought I saw you standing there looking at the Valley of the Nam."

Renni Nam said, "Yes, and I have seen you walking the hills, looking at the stars, no doubt contemplating the world as you know it. You were like that as a child. Now you are a grown man, and I have been expecting you. I had thought that you would come before now. Such a one as you must have

42

found it difficult not taking responsibility for yourself. These words stung Namuh. **All those times he had thought I should, could or would have done something sprang to mind.**

Renni Nam continued, "But you're here in the mountains looking for answers I suppose. I remember you as one who was always looking for answers. No child ever asked me so many questions. There is a time for questions and there is a time for action. The time for action is upon you. After all, you are here. Anyway, go ahead with your questions."

Namuh began haltingly to tell his tale. As he continued, the words poured out one on top of the other. Rapidly he told of the dream, the meeting with the Council and his house arrest. He told Renni Nam that he could never go back to the Valley of the Nam. The despair was evident in his words, and tears flowed from his eyes as he thought of the family left behind that he would never see again. Namuh had pictured the worst and already believed there was no hope for him or the Nam people.

Renni Nam listened quietly and at length, when Namuh was finished, rose to pace the floor of his hut. Namuh was physically and mentally exhausted and leaned back in the chair, but he was excited by Renni Nam's first words. "You must know, Namuh, that in every failure, in every instance when we think all is lost, there is the seed for great achievements."

Renni Nam was silent, letting this sink in, and then he began to speak, only barely concealing his own excitement. He told Namuh it was not Pilot speaking within him in the dream. He said, "I know you will not understand this, but it is important that you follow the lead of the spirit who came to you."

He went on, "The Universal Laws of God will be revealed to you by the following of the speaker within, the one in the dream. The revelation of these Laws is the most important thing because they are the very rules of life. He did say these laws would be revealed to you in the house?" "Yes", said Namuh. Renni Nam continued, "Then the permission to build the house must be your first objective. **If you concern yourself with what they can do** to you or on any negative aspect of your situation, your attention will be diverted from this first objective."

This was something Namuh would never forget. Renni Nam continued, "All focus must be on building the house. **These Laws are not something you will understand by the naming or telling of them by me but by the living experience of them.**" Namuh thought that this was a truth he recognized. It seemed to him that this was something he knew and understood.

Renni Nam said, "As you follow the instructions given to you, the house will reveal the Laws by the experiences you will have. You must not be afraid to return to the valley. **You must find a way to banish fear which is your greatest enemy.**" Namuh's father had told him this when he was still a child, and he knew the truth of it. Renni Nam then asked, "Would you rather remain here with me and never see your family again?"

Namuh wondered aloud, "What will I say to the Crew Elders? How can I make them understand that building the house is something I must do? What can I say that will convince them to allow me to proceed"? Renni Nam answered, "You followed the Law and told them everything that you could remember about the dream. What you did was not what you meant to do. You set off alarm bells everywhere because everyone hears with his own ears. We all think in pictures. A word creates pictures in our minds. If you say the word 'God', it will create a number of different pictures, a different one for each listener. Even among the Crew Elders, their pictures will not be the same. You must communicate by speaking to their understanding of the terms you use."

Renni Nam paced the floor of the hut. He continued, "When you told them that God would reveal 'Laws' to you in the house, they saw Pilot revealing new Laws like those commands in the Log. However, the Laws you were told that would be revealed in the house are of a different nature. These are the Laws that underwrite all laws, even those of nature. They simply cannot see Pilot giving new laws such as can be found in the Log to one who is not a Crew Elder."

Namuh struggled within his weary mind and body. He knew the dangers he faced, but he **thought** *he would rather die trying than remain isolated so close and never see his family again. He also wondered if he would be allowed to live if he did not obey God and build the house.* He thought a long time and said, "I am sure that if I was here with you, I could learn much, but sorrow would be heavy in my heart. It is not just that I would never again see my family, but I would not be fulfilling the instructions of God."

It was as if a great burden was lifted. He was no longer afraid. It was not as if Renni Nam had revealed a solution, but that he had allowed Namuh to look further within himself and determine that there was no answer but to follow the instructions of the "speaker within" as Renni Nam had called him.

If he was only imagining the events of the dream, he could be of no danger to the Crew Elders. Maybe he could convince them that he was not a danger to the Nam people. He would have to make them see this. If the dream was a true revelation of God, then the events would be fulfilled, and he had nothing to fear. If not, he would have to remove any fear that they might have of him. There was nothing to fear but his own fear. Maybe he could convince them of this truth and the benefits to them of banishing fear.

Renni Nam talked on through the day and into the night. He spoke of the Universal Laws and referred to God as Universal Being, the force within all life. When Namuh asked if God's name was Efil, Renni Nam said that such a force as Universal Being could hardly be named. "I have used the name because this force we call God is in all life, indeed in all matter, and all life is an expression of Universal Being." He told Namuh that his dream had been a revelation of his inner being. The answers had been given to him by his inner being because of his contemplative nature and his sincere desire to know himself and understand God. The answers were not given to him as a set of rules, but they would lead to understanding of these Laws.

45

With the approaching light of day, Renni Nam stopped talking, and Namuh fell exhausted into a restless sleep. Renni Nam did not disturb him until the sun was high and prepared a meal of hot Wonk and Feileb from the garden. Over this repast, Namuh asked about this little valley. He said, "No one in Nam could have imagined such a valley up here in the mountains." Renni Nam laughed and said, "There are many things the people of Nam have a hard time imagining. They once sought a pass through the mountains until the advent of Pilot. Then they quit searching. There are many such valleys within these mountains, and on the other side, there are places where there are no mountains."

Namuh stopped eating. He couldn't imagine a place where there was so much space and no mountains. Renni Nam continued, "There are many passes from which one can go through to the other side, but the closest is from here in this little valley. It is not even hidden. You were looking for me and were not looking for a pass, but you can walk a short distance through a tunnel behind this house and see a whole new world." *Namuh remembered what he had seen in the dream.*

Renni Nam lead him through the back of the hut into a dark tunnel. There was no need for a candle because they could see a bright light in the distance. When they came out, the light was so bright and the sun so warm that Namuh could not believe it. The cold on the climb had been severe, and in the valley where Renni Nam lived, it was not so warm.

When his eyes adjusted to the brightness of the day, he could see the valley below and what appeared to be even more valleys between the mountain ranges. It was the same as what he had seen in the dream. Renni Nam said, "You have no time to concern yourself with this now as you have much to do in the Valley of Nam, but some day you will lead others back to this valley and to new worlds. When you build the house, all things will become clear."

Namuh was greatly cheered by the words, "When you build the house." This meant that Renni Nam had no doubts that he would be allowed to build the house. *He wished he had the same confidence, but because of Renni Nam, he was becoming more certain that this was the purpose he had sought and that he could accomplish what God had told him to do.*

Namuh said his farewells, thanking Renni Nam for his understanding and words of wisdom. He returned to the ledge to begin his descent. It would be just as dangerous as the climb but this time his destination was one he knew. He was going home. Renni Nam had waved to him as if he was simply passing his house in the valley and returned to his work in the field.

Maybe, Namuh thought, *there was a reason for Renni Nam remaining here. After all, if I had not found Renni Nam, what would I have done? How would I have gained the strength for what lies before me? It was as if Renni Nam was there waiting to be called when he was needed, yet to get to him, I had to leave all that I love and make the perilous journey into the unknown. I had to have seen him in the moonlight and believed he was here. I had to be forced into a situation to make a climb of faith.*

CHAPTER TEN

NAMUH'S PREPARATION

On the one hand, Namuh was greatly relieved but he was returning home as puzzled about what he should say and do as he had been when he left to find Renni Nam. The words of Renni Nam were amazing, but how would he convince the Crew Elders? He was convinced that Renni Nam knew what should be done, and he had given Namuh some specific instructions. Renni Nam knew what the dream meant. At least he did not think Namuh was crazy, but Namuh thought *it might be much easier said than done*.

Namuh thought about what he would say and to whom he would be making his appeal. *He considered Worran to be thoughtful and rational, if not one of great wisdom, but Raef was different. He was everywhere, and no one knew when he would suddenly appear nor what he might do. He was, Namuh thought, an ever-present dark shadow that the brightest day could not disperse*. Many feared Regna, and her sometimes-violent actions, but it was Raef, quiet, sullen and manipulative, who moved her to action. It was Raef who the Crew Elders were afraid of. He would one day be Navigator, and no one wanted to cross him.

Namuh wondered what would befall the Nam should Raef become the Navigator. He could hardly imagine what it would be like. Raef and Regna - it was too much! He didn't want to think about it. God had said it would not happen. That would have to be enough for Namuh. After all, there was little he could do about the succession to Navigator. Namuh berated himself, **"Why are you wasting time thinking about who will be Navigator? You have more immediate worries."** He tried to concentrate on Worran and his approach to the old Navigator.

On the few occasions Namuh had been around Worran, he had seemed very reserved. Maybe this is because he is so old. It was as if he was a shell, but at least he was a passive sort of presence. It was Raef who exposed those who were not diligent in their worship of Pilot. It was "Raef who constantly spoke of the dire results of disobedience. It was always a picture of Missile coming in fire and devastation upon those who did not follow the Law of the Log that Raef spoke of. There he was, Namuh thought, worrying about Raef again. He just couldn't focus on what he had to do. Renni Nam had said it, and Namuh knew it was true. If you focus on the problem, the problem will grow. If you focus on the results you want to achieve, they will be manifested.

Even as he tried to focus on Worran and his presentation to the Council, Namuh's mind wandered back to Raef. He saw little difference in those Raef had exposed transgressing the Law of the Log as opposed to all the other Nam. He thought Raef must see and know more than the other Crew Elders. He was the one who had moved against Renni Nam, and Namuh thought it was because of his fear of the love and respect the teacher had attracted.

Raef was the one who defended the Law of the Log so fervently, and he used it to his own end. Maybe it was his fear that drove him to seek power over the Nam. Renni Nam had said that fear was the enemy that must be defeated.

Finally, Namuh, with almost Super Nam strength, managed to turn his thoughts to the positive steps he could take in convincing the Crew Elders to allow him to build the house that God had told him to build. He decided his appeal would have to be directed to Worran as if he alone was in the room.

It was Raef who was his enemy and the enemy of the Nam, and he would have to overcome his fear of Raef. Namuh felt that nothing he could possibly say would convince Raef. Namuh would have to rely on his knowledge of the Law of the Log and the logic of the Crew Elders. He would state his case without fear and appeal to Worran, the great interpreter of the Law.

Still he wondered what made Raef want the power that would come with being Navigator. Maybe he was just afraid. Namuh's father had told him, when he was young and being threatened daily by a bully, that the bully acted the way he did because he was afraid. "It is the way", his father had said, "for the bully to protect himself." Maybe Raef's fear drove him to seek power and impose his will.

What about Regna? Maybe her outbursts were just a way of handling fear. He supposed everyone feared something, but these two had more than their share. *I can only remove the cause of the fear or make them fear something much more than they fear me*. Ah! It was the first time it had occurred to him that maybe it was him they were afraid of. But why should they fear him?

They had been afraid of Renni Nam, but Renni Nam was a great teacher. He had wielded influence and was revered by his students. I am only a farmer with no desire to threaten the positions of the Crew Elders. He thought, *maybe they see me as someone who can see through them!* He had never breathed a word to anyone except Etam about his concern for the People of Nam should Raef become Navigator. *Maybe, with his powers as a Crew Elder, Raef could read Namuh's mind, or maybe there was a faculty of mind that allowed one Nam to intuitively know something of the inner person of those with whom he came in contact.* It was a new thought for Namuh. He wished that he had the time to contemplate this matter on the hillside, but he had to watch his step. It was a long and dangerous descent down the mountain, back to the hillside and his home.

By the time he neared his home, Namuh had decided what he would do and say. He would go back to the Crew Elders and tell them that while he respected them and their wishes, he simply must obey the instructions of, as Renni Nam had said, "the spirit within". Whether this was Pilot, Efil or a god by any other name, he must complete the mission that was given to him.

Suppose he did not build the house. Wouldn't this god punish him? And if he was wrong about what was wanted, what harm would be done in building a house? Renni Nam had said the one in his dream was not Pilot, but it would not do to complicate the situation in which he found himself. Renni Nam had said that he must communicate with them in a manner they could understand.

He arrived home and seeing the sleeping guard at the gate, returned to the house through the back door. Obviously, his absence had gone unnoticed. His family quietly embraced him, and he went to bed with a lighter but still troubled heart. At least he had a plan of sorts. He would think long and hard on his words even if he had to go out to the hillside to contemplate the evening before the hearing. He would have one more day to compose his thoughts, *and his fate would be in the hands of God, not the Council, Raef or even Worran.* This thought gave him courage to face the ordeal.

CHAPTER ELEVEN

NAMUH'S DEFENSE

Namuh appeared before the Council at the appointed time composed and less fearful than he imagined he could be under such circumstances. He had continually reminded himself of the alternative and the words of Renni Nam. *He recognized that this had been his decision.* Renni Nam had said that he must find a way to banish fear as it was his greatest enemy.

The choice to remain in the mountains or return to the valley had been his. He could have chosen safety but at what cost? He had decided there in the hut that his only real choice was to build the House for God. *Once this choice was made, why be afraid?* As he had dwelled on this decision, both on the way home and the following day, the fact that he had been forced to make this decision gave him further resolve to return the favor. Let the Crew Elders and Worran make the choice.

He spoke quietly but firmly to the Council. He told them again of the dream. He stressed the fact that he was a simple farmer and had followed the law as he understood it. It was, to the best of his knowledge, not his imagination nor was it something he had discussed with anyone but the Crew Elders. He had immediately requested the audience of the Council. He stressed his fear of Pilot if he did not obey his commands. He further expressed his concerns for the people of the valley if he somehow failed Pilot.

He reminded them of the fearful stories of the anger and immediate death of those who did not obey Pilot, and as he spoke, he gained courage. He reminded them of their stories and used their own beliefs to make his point. As for himself, he was now very unsure of the stories, but he knew them well and thought the Crew Elders, at least Worran, must believe them.

He reminded the Crew elders that he had always fulfilled his duties and never went to the hillside with anything left undone. He was not one who shirked his duties and had never tried to leave the valley. He had always shown respect to the Crew Elders and would show no disrespect now. However, Pilot had told him to build Him a house. What if he failed? He restated his loyalty to all Nam and the Crew Elders, but he reaffirmed that he must build Pilot's house.

Then Raef spoke ominously of the dangers that the building of such a house would bring to the valley. He argued that the worst sin of all would be for the Nam to start visualizing God. Everyone would have his own interpretation of what God looked like and what He wanted. Everyone would be trying to strike his own deal with God, and eventually the power of the Crew Elders would be eroded.

For peace and order to exist, there had to be respect and discipline. "The Great God Pilot," he said, "was a fearful God, a War God, a God of discipline, and he would discipline the people of Nam by allowing Missile to destroy them." He declared, "There will be grave consequences if Namuh is allowed to build this house."

Regna could not enter the Council Chamber, but she could be heard outside shrilly denouncing "the tale Namuh had told". She was angry like no one had seen her before. The veins in her neck stood out, and her face was purple in her rage. She told the Nam, "Demand of the Council that Namuh be put to death at once! His actions will bring on the end for the Valley of the Nam. Pilot will know as he knows everything. He will come again in the Great Bird and unleash Missile to destroy the Nam and everything in the valley. He will allow this calamity to come upon us with flame and fire, taking vengeance on one and all."

She said, "Instead of taking them to the valley without winters, Pilot will destroy us all as he destroyed those who disobeyed Him when He came so long ago." She reminded them, "Pilot need only stretch forth his hand, and the Nam died

53

instantly. The destruction caused by Missile will be much greater because Pilot, in his love, disciplines the people, but the coming of Missile will mean total destruction." She said, "This tale of Namuh's is blasphemy, and he cannot be allowed to live."

Inside, Raef questioned Namuh further, "You say Pilot told you all this in a dream? This was your dream. No one else can confirm this. Aren't you making this up to improve your mission in life? What do you hope to gain? Do you want to become a Crew Elder or aspire to be the Navigator? Only the Navigator has direct access to the Great God Pilot, yet you," he said disparagingly, "claim he has come to you, a farmer, while you dreamed on the hillside.

He continued. Do you want to lead the Nam into a new religion, after a strange god like Renni Nam tried to do? You are certainly talking about strange new laws which are against the traditions of Pilot and the people of Nam."

Namuh replied, "It was my dream, and it is true that none of you apparently experienced it with me. When I came to reveal the experience to you as I am required by Law to do, I thought that you as Crew Elders might already be aware of my experience. It was my dream, but since when have I been known as a liar in the Valley of Nam? I once aspired to be a student of Worran only because I wanted to learn more than was taught in the classes as a child. This was because of my sincere desire to learn more of Pilot and my respect for the Crew Elders, but the ambition to be a student of Worran passed with my youth."

"I am a simple man and derive much satisfaction from my work and my family. I value the time to walk alone on the hillside. I could do none of this if I had the duties of a Crew Elder. What have I to gain? Whatever I might gain, Pilot would give, not you or the people of Nam. However, if I do not follow the instructions I've received, I could forfeit my life and those who have stood in the way as well as the Nam people could lose everything."

"If I build the house, how will it harm the people? How will it go against the Law of the Log? If I, and those who might volunteer to help me, expend our resources on the house, where is the harm to the people? Regardless of what happens, there will be no harm to anyone. I will use the stone from the mountain near my home and the land I farm. There will be no cost to the Council nor will there be need for contributions from the Nam people as a whole."

He continued, "If I do not build the house, and it was Pilot in the dream, what would happen to me and to the Council? If it was Him, and you kept me from building the house, with whom will He be most angry, with me or with you? Might he not kill us as before? Might He not choose another Navigator?" Worran stood up quickly but said nothing. Namuh went on, "Is Pilot impotent, or might he find new Crew Elders?" At this point, all of the Council members were on their feet clamoring for the rebuke of Namuh by Worran.

Namuh raised his hands saying, "Please hear me out. My comments are made without disrespect to you. I am a man who has done his duty, fulfilling his "mission" as has been revealed by the Crew Elders of old. I have sought no other "mission" including the building of a house. I do not want to build a house, and I may have to build this one alone. What if I do not build this house? Will you not be responsible to Pilot? Remember, as the Law states that I must do, I brought this communication directly to the Council."

Finally, Namuh closed his appeal with what he thought was his strongest argument. "This is not a trial of Namuh. How do you know that this is not Pilot's trial of you? This is not a matter that concerns Namuh. It is a matter for you to decide. I would be happy to return to my family and the fields. I would be most at ease with my time alone on the hillside. I will comply with your decision in this matter. I am afraid of what Pilot might do if I disobey him, but you, the Council, are the representatives of Pilot. I must do as you say. I have obeyed the law and await your decision."

The Council was silent. It was as if the Council members were turning Namuh's words over in their heads to view them from an angle that had never before occurred to them. The demands for his death or banishment had ceased. No one else stood up to speak. There were none who moved to question him. Even Raef was quiet and seemed to be considering his argument. It was as if they were in shock, and Namuh knew this could not last. He had never lost eye contact with Worran, and he had said his piece. He must leave them to their considerations.

Namuh had never before felt so sure of himself. It was as if the words had been placed in his mouth. Renni Nam could not have been any more eloquent. There had been no hesitation, yet he remembered no occasion when he had spoken with such certainty or power. Always before he had avoided speaking in public, and he had never had reason nor the privilege of addressing the Council. In fact, he had never spoken to personages of such a high position in the valley. He was much happier on the hillside alone with the stars.

He did not believe it was the fierce Great God Pilot in his dream, but only by speaking to their way of thinking could he hope to accomplish what he knew was his mission. There was nothing more to be said. **If God wants the house built and my dream is true, they will leave me alone to build it. If this dream is only a fantasy, I will be killed or banished as a "No Nam".**

He watched closely the faces of the Council and the Crew Elders present for a sign. Again he looked to Worran who seemed to be deep in thought. Seeing nothing but bewilderment from the Crew Elders, he walked slowly from the Chamber.

CHAPTER TWELVE

THE COUNCIL'S DECISION

The discussions continued inside after Namuh had left. One after another of the Crew Elders addressed the Council. It seemed they had regained their composure and returned to the current fears that possessed them. Some were still for public condemnation of Namuh for the crime of blasphemy. They asked, "How could he dare speak to us in this manner and even suppose such events?"

Others argued for the banishment of Namuh as a "No Nam". They said, "Even if he can do no harm to the Nam and even if he does not intend to challenge our traditions, it would be dangerous to let him build such a house as he describes." No one spoke for Namuh, and no one wanted to let him build the house. All eyes were on Raef.

Raef spoke up saying, "It is all nonsense, and Namuh's continued existence should not be allowed. It can only lead to trouble. What good can come out of allowing the construction of such a house, and if we allow it, how will it effect the Nam?" Regardless of whether we allow the construction of the house or not, Namuh will continue to mouth his blasphemes against Pilot."

He said, "Simply by claiming that Pilot came to him and gave this command is blasphemy." "No.", he said, "We must strike down this sort of thinking and make an example of this upstart from the fields. He is uneducated and uninitiated in the advanced teachings of the Law of the Log. His words and actions are a danger to our traditions and our very existence. Should the Great God Pilot become aware of him and our refusal to punish him severely, I have no doubt that He will bring a great calamity upon us."

57

Amrak, one of the most respected of the Crew Elders, and the only one who might have been considered a rival to Raef for the position of Navigator, had been silent. Amrak was known to be the fairest and most balanced in his approach to the Law of the Log and the people of Nam. He did not approve of Raef's severe adherence to the Law of the Log nor his reliance on fear to control the people. They had often clashed over points of the Law but in spite of their differences, there never seemed to be any outward personal conflict. Amrak did not appear to aspire to the position of Navigator.

The Council members were quiet and expectant as Amrak rose to speak. Only Regna could be heard outside continuing her condemnation of Namuh as an enemy of the people and the forerunner of the valley's destruction. Worran sent the guard to the door with the command to her from the Navigator himself to "cease speaking immediately."

It was as if he had struck Raef across the mouth in public. Raef immediately left the Chamber and the Council members were amazed by his abrupt departure. They all wondered what this might mean to the succession. Until this moment there had never been in their mind any doubt about the eventual rise of Raef to Navigator.

Amrak spoke in a calm and reasonable manner. He was known to be a strong adherent to the Law of the Log but not such a zealot as Raef. All took his opinions seriously. He told the Council, "I share your concerns, but you should remain calm. Maybe the Great God Pilot is testing us and maybe this is an opportunity to prove to the Nam that only we are the representatives of the Great God Pilot."

He said, "Namuh has always been a dutiful man, and his conviction that God has told him to build a house for him, while a delusion, is harmless. We cannot take the blood of this simple man upon our heads. That kind of thing might truly bring the vengeance of the Great God Pilot upon us." He made no mention of Raef, but his words showed disapproval of the action as proposed by him.

Finally, Worran rose and all became quiet, waiting for his words and his pronouncement of sentence. The Council was hushed with anticipation despite their certainty that Namuh would be dealt with severely. Worran surveyed the assembly and then began speaking at his melodious best. He appeared to look each in the eye before speaking. "To some degree, I share the concerns of Raef, but in general I concur with Amrak's view. Namuh came directly to the Council and revealed his dream. If Namuh had not followed the Law, we might deal with him more severely."

He paused before continuing. "He is known as a bit of a dreamer, and many think him a little strange at best. If he was a troublemaker or had not been in compliance with the Law of the Log, revealing his dream openly to us, we could have and would have been obliged to stone him for blaspheming against the Great God Pilot. You are justified in your concern that Namuh's crazy, new thinking must not be allowed to infect the Nam people. This could cause all the Nam to start imagining conversations with the Great God Pilot."

He continued, "These strange new Laws that Pilot is supposed to reveal in the house is another matter, and Namuh must be warned of the danger of such heresy. However, as long as Namuh fulfills his duties, there will be little harm in his construction of a house. When the Great God Pilot does not come to the house, even Namuh will be forced to realize it was a dream of no importance. This will reinforce in the minds of all the Nam that to know the will of Pilot, one must come to the Crew Elders, and to the final authority - The Navigator."

Again he paused before making pronouncement on the matter. "As long as Namuh does not go too far and start teaching strange new laws, he will be allowed to build the house. We know that new laws cannot be coming from Pilot to one who is not a Crew Elder. We can in no way allow the traditional teachings as prescribed in the Law of the Log to be compromised. Anything not found in the Great Log is heresy.

However, I am confident that in the end, this episode will further unite the Nam people behind us."

Worran had spoken, and there could be no action taken which might bring his wrath down upon them. Everyone knew what the Great God Pilot could do, and Worran was His voice in the Valley of Nam.

CHAPTER THIRTEEN

NAMUH'S FOLLY

When Worran's decision was announced in the village, the news was accepted with quiet unease among the people. It was not that any had wished Namuh ill will, but the reason for the Council's decision was hard for them to fathom.

Already the news was out of a possible rift between Worran and Raef. It was no secret that Raef opposed the building of the house, and everyone knew he was a force to be reckoned with. It would be a dangerous course to get involved with a dispute in which Raef was a protagonist. It was reported that Worran had sent someone to silence Regna. It did not bode well that Raef was angry. They would have to listen to more lessons on the punishment that could come upon them, and he would be more ruthless. Sooner or later, Raef would be the Navigator, and his discipline would be harsh.

They were unaccustomed to thinking about such things, and the workings of the Council were a mystery to them. In addition to this, they had been conditioned not to dwell on complicated considerations. That was the duty of the Crew Elders. They were the representatives of Pilot, and it was their responsibility to determine the will of Pilot. It was their place to reveal His will to the Nam people. It was not for them to question the Crew Elders or their decisions. All they knew was that Worran's word was law, and Namuh would be allowed to build the house.

It had been revealed that Worran and the Council would allow the building of the house. The Crew Elders made it plain that the fact that Namuh was allowed to build the house was not necessarily a sign of Pilot's approval. In other words, there was no corroboration by revelation through Worran that this command had been given to Namuh. It was the delusions of

Namuh, and the Crew Elders did not unjustly punish one who was not fully responsible for his actions. He would be tolerated and would be allowed to build the house if he wanted to waste his time and resources.

In the village, Namuh confirmed that he would be building the house as instructed in his dream. He asked if there were any among them who would like to assist him or make contributions to the construction. He told them that he was proud that he had been given this honor, but the main consideration was not who was to build the house, but the end result that had been promised. He stressed that Pilot had told him to build a house for Him and the feast or famine cycle would be broken.

He explained that Pilot had told him in the dream to build Him a house and that the Crew Elders had agreed that the wise thing to do was comply. But when he described the house he was to build, all refused to be involved. They were afraid of the Crew Elders and could make no sense of such a house anyway. Poor Namuh, they thought, had finally broken under the strain of his father's death.

Everyone knew that his father's death had hit him hard. He had roamed the hillside until he had lost his mind. Everyone knew about how he sat out under the stars talking to the wind. Pilot did not, at least he had never before, talked to a Nam in a dream. The Great Log simply promised that Pilot would return and take all of them to the valley with no winters, and that was that!

As for Namuh's efforts, they were virtually forgotten until the structure climbed above the horizon unlike anything that had ever been seen in the valley before. Almost every Nam came at one time or another, as it was hard to resist a close look. Some came to gawk and some to jeer.

Namuh patiently explained to one and all that Pilot had told him to build this house for Him. "He has promised", Namuh said, "to break the cycle of winter suffering and provide Wonk so we can look above and past survival, see the beauty of the valley and maybe even see what is on the other side of the mountains encircling the valley."

"But we have the temple of the Great Bird at the far end of the valley." They said, "We go when we are there for the festival. We don't need such a strange thing here so near the village. It is ugly and looks like Missile, the evil one, that the Great Log warned us against."

While Raef would not go near the house nor in anyway contravene Worran's instructions, Regna frequently was among the curious who came to see the progress made on the construction. Regna said, "It is ugly and looks exactly like the pictures of Missile which Pilot had left behind. It was Missile who fought against Pilot, and he will be the one who will come to this house - not Pilot."

They went away shaking their heads, many feeling sorry for poor Namuh. What of his wife and children? Here he is spending all of their sustenance on stone and all of his time on a monstrosity with no purpose. Etam, Namuh's wife, could do little but watch Namuh's efforts and worry about the affects of recent events on their children, Hturt and Ynomrah.

Hturt helped his father when they finished their work in the fields. Ynomrah was intrigued by the construction and pitched in as if she too was an adult part of the team. Ynomrah was very young but knew her father to be an honorable and truthful man. If he said Pilot had told him to build Him a house, it must be true. It was an exciting and wonderful experience to see the house for Pilot take form right here on the hillside near their home.

It was back breaking work. There was plenty of stone on the hillside, and due to the fact that Namuh lived so close to the forest and mountains, building material was readily available. However, getting the stone to the site and getting it into place was a different matter.

Slowly it rose like a great stone tree without limbs; a huge pillar standing alone many times larger than the pillars of the temple. There was no place in the valley from which one could not see it. "Surely", said many of the Nam, "Pilot will be offended by this symbol of Nam stupidity." Others were intrigued by the structure simply because no one had ever seen such a thing. They thought it might fall down in the first, strong wind of winter.

Regna repeated to one and all her accusation, "There is no question that this is the work of Missile. It looks like Missile to the point that it is a virtual statue of the evil one himself. It is a monument to the enemy of Pilot."

CHAPTER FOURTEEN

FEAR AND DOUBT

When the house for God was finished, Namuh felt little pride in it. The work had been hard and was in addition to his field work as well as home garden. The constant derision from the Nam people had brought sorrow and stress into his life. He was unaccustomed to both. He was happy only that he had done what God had told him to do. Renni Nam had not said anything about what he should do now, only that the Laws would be revealed in the house. God had said this in the dream and as yet he had not seen God again nor seen any Laws revealed.

Harvest time was upon them, and other things would now have to occupy his time. Too long he had been preoccupied by the project and to some degree he knew his family felt neglected. They had all worked on the structure but he had been so concerned that the house be completed so God would come that he knew he had not been good company.

Not once had he failed in his duty to the people of the valley or his family. In spite of his clear recollection of the visit on the hillside and his trip up to Renni Nam's valley, he felt unsure of what he had accomplished. The house was not very pretty, ***and he could see no possible reason why God should want such a house. The whole of the valley thought him crazy. He would say nothing more; just go to the harvest and do his share***.

Every day when he returned from the fields, he would go up the hill and walk around the house he had built for God. Everyday he waited for a sign. He heard only the whispers and snickers of the villagers when he passed. Occasionally, someone would ask if Pilot liked the new house or if the Great Bird was going to roost on it. They wanted to know if Namuh had any new revelations. Some called it "The Holey House" because of the hole that was said to be in the roof.

The year's harvest was more bountiful than ever. The village square was filled to the point of being impassable. If there had been a way to exchange it with traders, it would have brought wealth to the village, but they knew nothing of such things.

It was not Pilot's will that the Nam be concerned with what the Crew Elders called abstract things. Did not the Great Log warn that the Nam must go in a straight pattern? Complex designs and charts were evil. Had not Pilot with his own hands drawn a large X, blood red, on the pictures of the evil one - Missile left behind with the Great Log? Had he not designated the Navigator to determine what was in the best interest of the Nam?

Months had passed since the house was finished. Still there had been no visit by God to inspect the work of Namuh. Whether God came from within, as Renni Nam said, or from another valley, as the Crew Elders said, He had shown no interest in the house.

Once it was finished, Namuh spent many hours in the house completing hundreds of details of the inner construction and then fussing over others he was unsure of. He had found the visit in the dream to be so startling that he was sure he had forgotten something important. He made changes and worked on minor things thinking that when the last detail was finished, this time God will find it complete and come to see the house for himself.

Regna had said the house was the work of Missile, and everyone knew that Regna said what Raef thought. If Raef had not been his enemy before, he certainly was now. Raef was no doubt planning some action against Namuh and the house, but Namuh knew it would not be a matter of a direct attack. Worran had spoken, and no action could be taken overtly by anyone against him. The specter of Raef was always present, however. Namuh could deal with this threat, but he wanted to allow Raef no opportunity to renew the attack.

Namuh was dejected and ashamed. *God had not come to the house that Namuh had built at such personal sacrifice. Maybe he had been fooled by Missile. The villagers said it looked like pictures of Missile in the Great Log. He had never seen the pictures, but why would they lie? Worse still, maybe it was just a dream with no significance. Maybe he was crazy.*

The courage he had gained by the trip to the mountains and the hearing before the Council was melting with time. Fear was again upon him. Namuh became bitter and more aloof. *Why had God embarrassed him this way?*

It was all well and good for Renni Nam to say that fear was his main enemy, but Raef was still there, and fear of Raef was not so easily removed from his mind. Raef was still a real threat. Namuh had created a powerful enemy and probably for no good reason. God had not come to the house, but its existence, without doubt, was viewed by Raef as a visible reminder of his embarrassment in the Council.

If Namuh could only prove that the dream was really the will of God or remove the house as a basis of Raef's concern, maybe things would get back to normal. If Raef did not see the house as a threat to his assumption of power as the next Navigator, maybe he would leave Namuh alone in the disgrace he felt so acutely.

Namuh again walked the hillside trying to come to some understanding of the events that had brought him to such circumstances. He gazed intently at the old mountain rising like a black wall, hoping to see a flicker of light from Renni Nam's fire. He wondered if the old man could see him. He knew he was there, not so very far away. If only he could talk with him again. He needed the strength of his wisdom and insight. Winter was coming. The nights were not so clear, and any hope of seeing him in the moonlight seemed to have passed with the clear fall evenings.

After a late night of contemplation, he went to bed with the same questions on his mind. He awoke with a start before sunrise. It was as if God had visited him again. He had the answer and now knew what to do. *He thought it strange how he could study a problem, which seemed to have no solution but could awake the next morning with a detailed answer to the problem including a plan of action.*

CHAPTER FIFTEEN

INTUITIVE THOUGHT

Namuh was anxious to talk to Worran about his plan. It had come to him as he slept, but he would not tell Worran that this idea had come from God. He had learned his lesson, and he would approach the Navigator in all humility with a possible solution to the wastage problem.

As Namuh approached the village to seek audience with Worran, his attention was attracted to two Crew Elders who were discussing the coming harvest festival. Every imaginable cake and dish in which Wonk was the main ingredient was to be prepared; every use their limited imaginations could come up with was suggested, for no one wanted to waste the huge stock of Wonk or to displease Pilot. "Even with ten festivals, and with all the Nam hauling away their allotment for themselves and their animals, much will rot on the ground", said one Crew Elder.

Namuh used this opportunity to broach the subject of his newly revealed plan. He told them that due to his situation, he had been reluctant to say anything but that he wished to make some use of the house which no doubt had been a mistake. He suggested that since Pilot had not come to the house he had built for Him, and since he had obviously mistaken the content of the dream and misinterpreted its meaning, they could use the house to store the unused Wonk.

This was a novel new thought for the Crew Elders. Namuh had to suffer their derision and their reminder of how foolish he had sounded at the Council hearing and how ridiculous the whole enterprise had been. Eventually, the Crew Elders allowed that the idea he had suggested might have some merit. They would talk to Worran about this idea, and if he approved, Namuh could have all of the Wonk he wanted.

Worran felt vindicated when told of Namuh's dejection and his offer to use the house he had built to store additional Wonk. He felt a little sorry for Namuh. Delusions could be powerful and costly to the one deluded. At the same time, he was convinced that the humiliation of Namuh could work to the advantage of the Crew Elders and the glory of Pilot. It would be a public admission of Namuh's delusions and even stupidity. The house he had built for Pilot would become a place to keep the Wonk that would go to waste. What could it hurt for Namuh to have the excess Wonk? It was as if they were throwing away the Wonk. Namuh's house will become a place to keep waste and, therefore, no more important than the pit at the lower point of the valley where all waste was dumped.

Namuh heard the grumbling though from some who were suspicious of his every action. "Namuh's god won't go hungry." And others said, "Missile will get it." Still others thought it was a waste of time hauling it out "to get wet in the Holey House." The Crew Elders thought it a great idea to use the house against Namuh. It served their purpose to say that the house was good for nothing but waste. Time was short, however, and each had to be busy before the winter came. Namuh could do what he liked with the left over Wonk, and may his house be filled with Mod. Namuh could have their blessings, but he could not have their help.

Mobilizing his immediate family, Etam, Hturt and Ynomrah, Namuh made trip after trip from the village to God's house, hauling the excess Wonk. Dimit helped in the evenings. He did not want to be seen there during the day. His watch-word was discretion as surely there was no need to offend the Crew Elders, especially Raef. It would only bring his wrath upon them once he became the Navigator.

Dimit loved Namuh. He had always been his friend, but sometimes he thought Namuh was just too bold. He was always an outsider, and there was no good reason to bring this kind of trouble upon himself. He was doing the prudent thing to try and make use of his mistake with the approval of the Crew Elders.

Using the pulley system Namuh had seen in the dream and designed for the house, he hoisted the Wonk and packed all he could into each floor. Only the top floor was left empty because of the opening there. He had, as yet, not built the hatch that could be closed against the wind and rain. It was hard work, but Hturt and Ynomrah were anxious to help their father. He had certainly had his share of abuse.

Only Namuh went to the upper floors and even he tended to keep his eyes averted from the view at the top. He seemed so sad and rarely talked with them as he had before the dream. They wished they could do more but knew that there was nothing to be done but help where they could.

All levels were so packed with Wonk that Namuh worried out loud that *"If God ever does come, there would be no room." There would be no room for the Great Bird,* Namuh thought, *but then God had not used the Great Bird when he took him to see the valleys on the other side of the mountain range. The Great Bird may not even exist, he thought. Maybe it was just a creation in the mind of the Crew Elders. Even if it was real, God obviously did not use it all the time. Renni Nam said it was not the same God but still Namuh could not quite visualize the God Renni Nam talked about.* He couldn't remember looking at him when he came in the dream. Namuh need not have worried because there was never any sign of the Great Bird, Pilot or the God he remembered in the dream.

Fall was past, and yet winter gave little warning of the severity to come. Work continued at a frantic pace, each Nam carrying in his heart the sure knowledge of the inevitable winter and the hardships it would bring. Each Nam family stored their allotment of Mod in their houses and sheds. Roofs were strengthened and food put up for the winter. Winter clothes were repaired, and fuel was stacked for the expected long winter nights. But no Nam had ever seen a winter like that poised in the mountains above.

71

CHAPTER SIXTEEN

THE RECKONING

Suddenly, it was upon them with such a fury many were still caught unprepared. The snow was heavy, and the wind howled like a monster out of the mountains. The Valley of Nam had experienced some long and harsh winters, but this one was immediately recognized as different. It wasn't just the fact that the snow was heavier, but this was accompanied by winds like they had never seen before. The wind was so high that the snow burned their exposed skin. It was not the typical heavy snow fall or weather front to which they had become somewhat accustomed.

Raef had warned of such a calamity. Both he and Regna had said that Pilot would punish them if Namuh were allowed to build the house. Maybe this fierce wind was the chastisement of Pilot and would be the end of the Nam. Many were frozen by more than the snow and wind. They were frozen with fear. If they attempted to escape the wrath of Pilot they might incur even greater punishment. If they waited with humility, the Crew Elders would no doubt come to their aid, and appeals for the mercy of Pilot might result in the cessation of the wind and their salvation.

It was difficult for the Nam to see even a few paces in front of them because the wind made the snow sting their faces. Soon houses could not be seen except for an occasional chimney. Sheds were blown away, Wonk and livestock scattered to the wind. Homeless and freezing, some began to move slowly toward the only thing they knew to be their possible place of safety, the house that Namuh had built.

All had been able to see it, no matter where they lived in the valley. Maybe this storm was the punishment of Pilot, and maybe this strange structure that Namuh had constructed on the hillside was Pilot's house. Survival was all that mattered. If they did not move, they would perish for lack of fuel and food. The house that had long been the object of their jokes was the only place to go.

Namuh and his family had moved to the house when the storm began. It was where the Wonk was as well as his animals. It was strong, and he knew that it could withstand the storm. There had been no thought in his mind that the Nam would come, but without hesitation, he opened the doors of the house for those who began to arrive. It seemed like an endless stream, but he knew it was only a small part of the people of Nam Valley.

Numbed by the cold and fearing for their lives, many failed to risk going out of their homes. Some had no ability to focus on the risk of non-action. Thoughts were limited to immediate survival. It was a storm without precedence, well beyond the Nam experience. Even the Crew Elders could not bring themselves to venture into the whirling mass of wind, ice and snow in order to minister to the people.

Tnetopmi and Yhtapa had not been seen. Everyone was either cowering in their huts or trying to make their way to the house that Namuh had built. Tnetopmi felt powerless to do anything. What could one Nam do against the elements? He might be King, but he was only one Nam. He could do nothing for the people of Nam or for himself.

"Where was Worran anyway?" he wondered out loud. His court was empty. No one had come to the palace for assistance or to entreat him to talk to the Crew Elders. Yhtapa did not seem to be bothered by the storm or the flight of the people toward the house Namuh had built. Everything would work out. Like Tnetopmi said, "What could they do?"

As more and more of the Nam arrived at the house, Namuh wondered where the Crew Elders and Raef were seeking shelter. Only Amrak had come and he had said little about what the Crew Elders might do. Where else could they go? Would they rather perish than come to the house? Still no other Crew Elders came, and many of the Nam made no move to escape to the house Namuh had built. As for the Crew Elders, Namuh thought, it would be like admitting that he was favored over them. Amrak appeared to be at home with the community in the house and was as helpful as he could be to Namuh. He had made no move to preach to them and had not suggested that the storm was the punishment of Pilot for their transgressions.

As for the Crew Elders, there had been no means to meet together, and Worran was not physically or mentally capable of rallying them. In fact, there had been no one to take the lead. Raef had maintained a low profile since he left the Council Chamber at Namuh's hearing. Amrak was one of the first to go to the house that Namuh had built, but they knew nothing of this.

Individually, the rank and file Crew Elder could not act without leadership. They were afraid to go and simply waited for instructions from Worran. Their presence in the house, each felt, would be like admitting that the Great God Pilot had talked to Namuh instead of to them through Worran. They were the ordained representatives of the Great God Pilot, yet they were stunned by the storm. Some felt that this was the calamity Raef warned would befall them if Namuh was allowed to build the house.

Worran felt old and very cold. Last winter he had wondered if he could make it through the long cold months, and this winter was already far worse. Regardless of what might happen, he would not leave his house. If it were time for him to die, he would die. He would not make another appearance until the storm was over, and he certainly would not go to the house that Namuh had built. That would be a humiliation that would kill him if the winter storm did not. Pilot would protect the Nam, and he was "Pilot's" Navigator. He would die that way.

Regna could hardly be seen in the midst of the storm, but she was there in what had been the road to the hillside. She was waving her arms against the movement of the Nam toward the house Namuh had built. Since no one could see or hear above the roar of the storm, little thought was given to her. Survival was all that mattered. No one feared her. She had simply become irrelevant.

Raef was nowhere to be seen. He fumed and cursed the storm as well as Namuh. He felt humiliated by Worran's rebuke of Regna, and at the same time blamed her for being the cause of the rebuke. He would weather the storm and then concern himself with the problem. Worran was old. Maybe he would not survive the storm, and if he didn't, Raef told himself that he knew how to take care of simpletons like Namuh. They would see that he, Raef, was the rightful heir to the position of Navigator. Once this was accomplished, he would make them pay. He would make them all pay. They would quake in their boots at his appearance like they did when he talked about the Great God Pilot. And yet, he knew that he was the one who was afraid now; so very, very afraid.

The road to the house was clearly visible once a Nam family made the attempt to escape to it. The march of those going to the house had created a path that could be followed. Even with all the snow and wind, the tracks could be followed. It was like a deep rut carved in the snowy landscape. There was no other movement in the valley, and it was the only sign of life. However, only those searching for a way could have seen it.

At the house, there was great relief at being alive, fear that loved ones could not be found, sorrow that some were already known to have perished and a great deal of confusion. The house was full of Wonk, and to a less degree, there was Feileb. It was big, warm and could provide quarters for many. "It is truly a gift from Pilot that the house is here", they said.

For the brave who were fiercely determined to survive, there was only the house that Namuh had built. He must have been right. Pilot had provided for their salvation. Sometimes Pilot's ways were far above their ways as the valley with no winters was far away. It was not easy to understand Pilot's purposes, but he had provided for them.

CHAPTER SEVENTEEN

THE HOLEY HOUSE IN THE STORM

The house that Namuh built stood like the mountains themselves against the storm, and it was warm. Due to Namuh and the agreement of the Crew Elders, it was full of Wonk. All the water they needed was available simply by melting snow. The hole in the roof was no hole at all but a very effective flue, and the warmth from the fires in the lower levels rose to warm those above. At first there was plenty of room, but as the Nam continued to come it had seemed that space would become a premium. Still, it was a big house and could hold even more Nam, should more come. It was a house filled with Mod!

For those who had fled the storm to the house, the immediate danger was over, but as always, the loss of one's home and possessions is hard to take. All were willing to accept the house that Namuh had built as their salvation, but no one wanted to take responsibility for their situation, nor for the house, which was now their home. They were still dazed by the severity of the storm and their brush with death. "This was punishment for something the Nam people had done wrong.," they said. Their common attitude was, "What can we do but accept the will of Pilot?"

One day, after listening to the complaints for some time, Namuh rose to speak. It was the first time he had spoken to so many at one time. He had not planned it, but he knew the purpose of the house was not to house complaints for God. He knew that while they had comparative safety in the house, survival of the Nam was still in the balance.

He said, "You have been so busy worrying about your houses down there in the valley that you have forgotten there are others who do not have the safety of the house, nor food in their bellies. What of the Crew Elders, Raef and Regna? What of our Navigator, Worran? He is old and will need assistance to get to this haven from the wind and cold. They are all of our blood and are children of the same God. We must at least let them know they are welcome among us. It is their responsibility to take the action necessary to save themselves, but it is our responsibility to try and find them. We must plan, we must share, for God has provided abundance for all."

It would be the last time he would speak to the community until moved to do so as he came to understand something of the Laws that were being revealed. Namuh did not see himself as a leader and had never sought such a role. His concern for those who had not found the safety of the house had overridden his natural shyness.

Those who had come were concerned with why they were being punished. They had not thought about the abundance of Wonk that had been provided. Namuh reminded them, "I have looked for a place to pray, but this house is so full of Wonk and people it seems we can take no more. Yet, how can we ignore or turn away our neighbors? We have an abundance of Wonk and a warm house. We must share with those who will listen and help themselves."

Namuh remembered a recent conversation with Ecnadnuba, known as Nuba, who he had placed in charge of the Wonk in the house. Nuba's duties made him responsible for the team that foraged for roots, fuel and catches of feileb that had frozen. Sometimes they were able to retrieve Wonk left by those who had died. They had already recovered many things that could contribute to their survival efforts.

When Namuh had commented on the rate at which they were consuming the Wonk, Nuba had been blunt. He said, "If the Crew Elders and the people of Nam had not been such fools, they would long ago have built houses like this to store Wonk for the winter." He had gone on to say, "There has always been an abundance of food and anything the Nam people needed. They simply had not known how to conserve it."

Of course Nuba had never been able to say such a thing publicly, and hindsight is much easier for most of us than future sight, but the seed had been planted in Namuh's mind. He marveled at the candor and openness of those who now sought to survive in the house. Nuba had said "abundance", and Namuh had thought that it was a great word. It meant "more than enough". Nuba was right. *There had always been plenty in the Valley of Nam. It had never been a matter of shortages. The problem had always been in the mind of the Nam people.*

Namuh had not built the house for the storage of Wonk. It was not a shelter for food or people, but it served this purpose well. Maybe it was all a part of what God had told him in the dream. *Maybe this was what God had been trying to tell him all along. Had he not said, "Build the house and you can break the cycle of starvation?"* Yes, this was a thought that would bear more thought.

Namuh summed up his thinking on the matter. "If we can just think this through, we can survive and save others." We must have a greater purpose than our own safety. While concern for the safety of your families required you to take responsibility for yourselves and make the difficult journey to the house, we must now put our comparative safety to good use." *Self preservation was necessary but this alone is not enough.*" This was the beginning of Namuh's understanding of the necessity for "Proper Perspective." It was a concept that Namuh knew would receive a great deal of his attention, but now he had to see to the formation of teams to fulfill their greater purpose.

There were plenty of volunteers, where only a short time before everyone had been concerned for his own losses and the punishment he had to bear. He told the volunteers, "This will entail some risk. We are safe here and have plenty of Wonk, but we will have to leave the comfort and safety of the house and cover the whole valley looking for those who will be saved."

First they had to find more space. They found space everywhere, much more than anyone thought was available. They stacked and moved, via the pulley through the shaft, all they could to the levels above. More of the Nam people could be brought to the house, but they had to find them and help them come. They could give help to those capable of receiving it, and the house would be open to all who would come.

Renni Nam had suggested that he follow the spirit of the dream. He had noted that *one cannot give to those incapable of receiving, nor could he receive what he was incapable of receiving. That would be like attempting to pour water from a large container into a small one. The problem with receiving was related directly to the capability to receive.* This seemed simple after he had thought about it. It must be one of the Laws both God and Renni Nam said he would experience. The other Laws were being revealed as well, but he would have to reflect further on them.

Once they had made room, Namuh was overcome with emotion. Tears of joy arose in him and a lightness that he had not felt since his talk with God in the dream, and later, his defense before the Council. He, Namuh, had the answer for the survival of his friends and neighbors. The way had been revealed. Now with understanding, he could act. Those without homes and stock could stay in God's house. There would be space and food. There was also the beginning of an idea. He knew now how all this could have been avoided. What had happened would never cause this devastation again.

CHAPTER EIGHTEEN

BONDING IN THE HOUSE

Closeness developed between Namuh and those who had come to live in the house. They recognized that it was not just this strange house but Namuh's idea and concern for the people of Nam that had made it possible for them to save themselves. Even those who had made fun of the strange structure with no windows began to look upon it as something special. Pilot may never use it, they thought, but it provided shelter for them and was truly a gift from Pilot to the Nam.

The community in the house had become very close. Even with a certain degree of crowding, there were few complaints. Those in the house had mutual survival in common. They had all lost family and friends to this fierce storm, but friendships that might never have materialized under normal circumstances had blossomed into love. There was genuine love for each other and mutual interdependence.

Evol was loved by one and all. Her very nature and the tireless way she went about helping anyone and everyone who needed her assistance had made her the one many turned to with their problems. She had become the mother figure of the house that Namuh had built. She was soft spoken and always seemed to have a heart full of joy and love for all.

When she was asked one evening about how she managed to maintain such an attitude of love with all that had happened to her family, she said, "It is true I have lost my whole family, and no one can replace them in my heart. However, in this house I have been blessed with an even larger family." She noted that she did not believe that they could have survived together or done anything had it not been for the growing love of the community in the house for each other and those who remained outside.

"Love is the glue", she said. "We needed shelter and food. We needed to help all those we could. We needed to recognize and learn from this terrible experience, but nothing would have been possible without this growing love between us and the expression of love we have seen Namuh and our leaders express here. By their tireless efforts on behalf of those still outside the house, they have shown love for their fellow Nam and even their enemies."

Namuh, on the landing above where some of the volunteers were gathered, sat listening to Evol. He had not analyzed his own actions. It had been a need within him that he had not questioned. This was not the time and place to even consider his near banishment or possible execution. There were still Nam people out there, and all that could be done to save them had to be done. That was that, and there was no question in his mind about the proper action of those in the house, though they had precious little materially to give. *If they gave of what they had including food and shelter, they gave life, and that was everything.*

He thought about what Evol had said which led him to thinking along these lines. *What could one give to another? When they gave food and shelter; or when they saved a life, what had they really given? Any action on behalf of another was, in fact, an expression of love. When you came right down to it, the only thing one could give to another was love. Love had to be the great abiding truth, the Law of God. This is a principal or truth that cannot be avoided. He decided right then that love had to be the most important of all the Laws of God, the one Renni Nam called Universal Being.*

Namuh had come to the realization that he had started all this even if he might have been mistaken about it being God's instructions. Still, he felt that the talk with God seemed so real and there were great lessons he was learning from the experience. If it had not been God, whatever the reason he was moved to act as he had, it had been a fortunate mistake. The house had already meant the salvation of many.

There was still much to be done, however, if more of the Nam were to be saved. *His thoughts centered on what they could do to find and give aid to more of those still out there exposed to the elements.* Many, no doubt, suffered from a lack of food and from the cold. It might be difficult for them to focus on how to provide for themselves and their families. No one had seen any of the Crew Elders except Amrak, and the leadership of Worran and Raef was not available to them. *They had to depend upon their own thinking and individually take responsibility for their actions. Recognition of this fact will see us through*, he thought.

Living in a storehouse of food, protected from the elements, bathing in the glow of love for one another, they grew stronger. They forgot their fear of the storm. If there were only more of these houses, all the Nam could have been saved and the fierce winters simply would not have been so fearful to the Nam people. With Namuh's help, they would go out to find those who had not found their way. A powerful need to share their good fortune rested on their shoulders.

As they consumed more of the Wonk, they moved into other levels of the house. There was plenty of food and space to share, and there was no fear of the elements. They could meet any challenge because of the house that Namuh had built.

Namuh considered his need to give, a phenomenon of the situation, but he knew that only with the giving could he and the others in the house have been blessed as they had been. This had to be one of the Universal Laws. How it fit with the other Laws was not clear to him, but he concentrated on just determining what the Laws were. He would learn how they were all related to each other and how they represented God when he understood more. He was happy with the thought, and that was enough for now.

CHAPTER NINETEEN

LESSONS ARE LEARNED

There was no lack of evidence that by working together, those in the house had been able to accomplish a great deal. The food, shelter and basics of survival were there in the house. Organizing and working together had saved many more. Those in the house were as diverse as they had been before coming to the house, but now they worked as one for the survival of the Nam people.

Nightly, the leaders of the teams Namuh had formed met around the fire on the fourth level to plan their activities. After each planning session, they lingered to discuss subjects that Namuh had never talked about with any Nam before the storm. He was both surprised by the familiarity of these leaders with problems he had been wrestling with and their points of view. It had rarely occurred to Namuh that others had been equally concerned with the future of the Nam and that others thought in the same manner as he. He was still reluctant to publicly discuss what Renni Nam had told him and mostly listened to their views, seldom making comments.

Namuh was drawn out of his reverie by Ytinu. She was speaking, and what she was saying had attracted his attention. She was a valued member of one of the teams that was making the house a great success. She had become a leader in the community out of pure insistence on her part that they work together. She had not been elected to a position of leadership but had worked tirelessly to settle disputes and to make cooperation and unity of purpose the main goals of the community.

"The individual is important", She said. "If it had not been for one individual, Namuh, there would have been no house. If he had not convinced the Crew Elders to let him take the excess

Wonk to the house, there would have been no food. If he had reacted in a negative way to those who had made fun of him, none would have gained entry to the house." *The individual was the important unit of the whole.* Namuh knew this but Ytinu, in her own quiet way, had expressed this thought daily to all those around her.

Recognition of the importance of each individual, and the fact that all were part of a greater whole, was not lost on Namuh. He had simply not conceptualized it much less talked about it. He knew what she said was true and knew also that this was one of the Laws he had been told would be revealed. This was not a new thought *as the need for unity was stressed in the Law of the Log. However, Ytinu stressed first the importance of the individual and then the role of the individual as part of a greater whole.*

Namuh had once discussed her favorite subject with her. He had asked her if she had ever thought about this subject before coming to the house. She said, "I often wondered how we could break the cycle of these harsh winters and solve our many problems without working together. It seemed logical to me, but I had no place in the leadership and, being a woman, did not have the opportunity or access to the Crew Elders. I once spoke of the question of unity and at the same time the importance of each individual to the Queen. She acknowledged that it was important to work together in every way, but she warned against talking about the importance of the individual because she said it would anger the Crew Elders."

Namuh said, "I never thought much about it until I went in search of Renni Nam. It was after I was placed under house arrest that I sought him out in the mountains. He talked about the Laws that were forever in place and that originated from Universal Being. He said that *these Universal Laws were the divine expression of Universal Being. One of these Laws he mentioned was called the Law of Absolute Unity. In other words, the life force in all living beings was part of the whole.*

Each is distinctly his own being, but all are a part of one whole."

Ytinu said, "I did not know you had found Renni Nam. I remember him from the campfires when I was still young. Before that, he had been a teacher in my school. Maybe it was from something he taught or maybe I just came to recognize that **we are all a part of a greater whole**. In any event, it is a concept that has grown within me because of my experiences here in the house." She left him then with his thoughts, saying, "We owe you a great deal Namuh, and I'm very happy that you are a part of our whole."

On another evening, Namuh had only been half listening to the conversation when one of the comments caught his attention. *He knew that his thinking had gone through a long process of change dating back to his childhood. It had been accelerated by the dream on the hillside and subsequent events. Everything had always been changing, but the development had been so slow that he supposed no one else had noticed either.*

At the same time, the teachings of the Crew Elders had seemed to go in the opposite direction from the thoughts of the people. The Crew Elders had become constantly more apocryphal. Their lessons consisted more of continual warnings about what Pilot was going to do rather than the principles of the Log. Namuh now knew *that Renni Nam had only been a part of the changes that had been coming all along.*

Evolution had been taking place with the Nam people, and Renni Nam had tried to provide the basis of what was to come. Namuh himself had become a catalyst in this process. Since the storm hit, and even while building the house, his own thinking had changed. This had seemed to him to be something that just happened. In retrospect, he thought, *nothing happens by accident. It was a Law, like the seasons, that was inevitable.*

Evlove was now speaking. She said, "Everything has been changing, and since the advent of the house, the changes have been more noticeable. **I think change is something all the**

Nam must acknowledge because it is a fact, but the problem is that we resist change. It is our resistance to change that causes us such pain." Namuh had said nothing, but the thought persisted. There was no arguing with the fact that nothing stayed the same, and he came to know this principle was a Universal Law.

Tcartta, (pronounced Cartta), spoke up now, and Namuh did not follow the connection of her comments to what Evlove had been saying. He thought maybe that while in his reverie, he had missed something. Tcartta related how she had been concerned only with survival when she first came to the house. She had been one of the first to come. She said she had thought that more would come though she knew some would not for many reasons. During the period of construction, she too had seen little use for the house and had thought Namuh crazy.

She said she had, however, been attracted to Namuh because of his sincerity and his desire to help the people of Nam. She said, **"When our purpose is greater than our individual selves and our individual desires, others are drawn to us. The resources that we require for this greater purpose become available as if by a great stroke of luck. Now I know it is more than luck. When our purpose and focus are great, we cannot help but attract whatever we need and attract in abundance."**

Evitcepsrep, whose nickname was Evit, began to relate how, after one grueling trip foraging and looking for survivors, she had come to realize that **how we think, act and react largely depends upon our perspective.** Evit had described the valley in the midst of the storm. She said, "It was not like visiting the village or even the place I had known from birth as my home. It was like another world. It bore no resemblance to the Valley of Nam."

She had gone on to describe the reaction of a family who would not allow them to help and had decided to remain in the village. What caught Namuh's attention was Evit's statement that **"It was all in the way we look at things."** She said, "In the view of this family, coming to the house would have the effect of making Pilot more angry than he already was. They were being punished, and to seek shelter in the house to them would have been an insult to Pilot. They could not see safety, shelter and food. They could only see the consequences of displeasing Pilot. *It was a matter of perspective."*

Namuh had thought to himself that this was self-evident. It was so simple that to repeat the thought seemed almost a waste of time, but the truth of it stuck with him, and he quietly moved away from the group. He had a powerful need to escape to a higher level of the house just to think about it.

A few days later, after the planning session, Etaler spoke of his family and friends who, either would not come or who could not be found. He had said that there should be more that those in the house could do. After all, those still in the valley were Nam as much as those in the house. As he talked, he seemed to ramble, touching on the dependence of the livestock on the Nam and how the Nam was dependent on the Wonk they raised for survival. Eventually he noted, dolefully, **"Every living thing was dependent on every other living thing."**

While Etaler had not expressed his thoughts coherently, it was not lost on Namuh. He had thought about this before, and Renni Nam, when Namuh had visited him, also had spoken about how **everyone and everything including Universal Being are connected**. Renni Nam had gone so far as to say, **"Every living thing possesses a life force that is the expression of Universal Being. He had said that it was not possible to separate God from life."**

As Namuh related the words of Renni Nam to Etaler and the others who had gathered by the fire, all were quiet. None spoke, and Etaler in particular seemed to absorb the thought. When those present moved away from the fire, Etaler followed Namuh asking more questions. To him, this one thought was like a flash of light in his mind. It was one that he took to heart, and in the years after their experience there in the house, it would be Etaler who taught the young about the relationship of all to all.

Namuh had been happy to see Amrak when he arrived at the house. He had always liked him though he had no real relationship with him. Long after he had been given permission to build the house, he had been told that Amrak had spoken in his defense at the Council hearing. He had never acted in the authoritarian way of the Crew Elders. He had always seemed to maintain harmony with everyone including his fellow Crew Elders. There had always been balance in his life. He never seemed to go overboard in anything he said or did. Amrak was one of those individuals who had never seemed radical in any way. He had shown respect to the Crew Elders and his fellow Nam.

Namuh thought that Amrak, while saying little, had expressed in the way he lived all that one needed to know about him. Namuh remembered that years before when the Nam had cut too many trees along the river, a lot of damage had been done to the fields. There had been flooding because the trees had provided a windbreak that suddenly was no longer there. The winds had stripped the top soil away, and the crops in that area had not been good until Amrak had lead in the effort to plant more trees.

Namuh remembered that at the time Amrak had said, **"The valley is like a finely tuned instrument. If any string is missing, it will affect the total."** Amrak had noted that nature would seek to balance the loss. He was successful in his efforts for which he was still remembered today.

Namuh had sought the council of Amrak with regard to the Crew Elders. It had been his thought that they should take a body of Nam and bring them to the house by force if necessary. After all, it would have been for their own good. Amrak had counseled against any such action. He said, "You do not want to become as we were, a militant force. You are not that kind of Nam, and those in the house, the survivors of Nam, are not searching for one to replace Worran. Whether they ever thought about it or not, the Crew Elders had been a yoke around their necks and are the instrument of the almost total destruction of the valley."

Namuh had been offended at the suggestion that he might attempt to assume power in the valley. That had been the furthest thought from his mind, but when he considered it, he realized that this was the way it had always been. *As long as he could remember, there had been someone who thought he knew better how everyone else should live than the people themselves could possibly know.* By assuming this role, he would be saying, "I know more about what is good for you than you yourself know. You have to be protected from yourself."

Amrak had gone on to say, **"There seems to be a perfect scale of justice in the natural order of things."** He said, "One would think that the wild and predatory animals are the best equipped for survival. They have claws, speed and power, yet for many years they seem to have been diminishing in number. On the other hand, sheep, which appear to have no capacity for survival, being docile and almost mindless when it comes to self-preservation, continue to grow in number. There are more sheep than ever before, at least there had been before the storm. They didn't have the weapons of the predators, but they bred much faster." Namuh knew that even the sheep that had been saved in the house would far outnumber the predators in the valley.

Amrak also noted that there had developed a harmony among the occupants of the house. In the events that had befallen them, there was a justice that went beyond what the Crew Elders called justice. He said, "God's justice and nature's justice are ultimately perfect."

Namuh had pondered this thought for days. At first he could see no justice in the loss of life from the storm but had come to the understanding that the physical laws of nature are like the Universal Laws. *They are unchangeable and in place for all. If the Nam had used their abundant assets, they could have lived in harmony with nature's laws.* If the Crew Elders would not come to the house, they would die. There was simple justice in this fact, and it was not one administered by him. The Crew Elders were welcome, but no force would be used.

CHAPTER TWENTY

UNDERSTANDING

One evening while pondering the meaning of their salvation in the house built for God, Namuh climbed up on the steps leading to still another level. He was thinking that soon they would need more room as the people continued to find their way to the house. All the people had to do was take action. The house had stood like a beacon in the valley before the storm. Now it was hard to see anything or any sign of life on the frozen waste that had been their homes and fields, but the path could be found and followed. He thought about this and stopped to consider the events of the past year.

Namuh was lost in thought and had paused to sit on the steps between the floors. He dozed against the wall listening to the wind through the opening to the shaft. One thing Namuh had enjoyed were the stories around the camp fires where he could picture in his mind the descriptions the Crew Elders were so adept at painting with words. He was thinking that some day the story of this house would be told.

He felt the presence of God with him and all around him. It was as if He had come to him and was inside his body. Namuh asked, "Why did you never come to this house I built for you?" "Oh but I have.", said a voice that seemed to come from somewhere inside his own head; but it said no more, and he awoke with a start.

Now, he knew that *there was more to this house than he had thought. God might never come to it, but it had a purpose. There was more to it than a place they had turned into a home and storage.* Every level he went up taught something new, each more exciting than the last - how to survive, save his friends and help others find their way to the house and more.

This house had proved to be God's house after all, and there were Laws of God being revealed in the house. There had been lessons learned and ever more to contemplate upon, but for Namuh, while the Universal Laws were becoming apparent, their depth of meaning was not fully understood.

He had begun to compare his experiences at each level he moved up in the house. It had occurred to him that ***at each level it was like a different state of mind or a different part of his mind.*** It was hard to describe what he was feeling, and he doubted if anyone would understand what he was talking about. He would keep his own counsel on the subject for the time being, but he recognized the changes in his own way of thinking.

He knew these experiences were teaching him many lessons, but he had been unable to associate all these experiences with the Laws that God had said would be revealed in the house. The lessons were experienced, and he had gained understanding but could not explain this to the community in the house. When he tried to talk about what he felt and what he was thinking, it sounded awkward and confusing. He would wait until he understood things fully. No. Renni Nam ***said it was a matter of experiencing them, and all his experience and understanding had come in the process and in relation to those who had come to the house. He would begin discussing his thoughts and feelings with the others***.

He longed for the hillside, which had been his refuge and place for thought, but the lessons he was learning were in the house and in relation to the Nam who had come. Each level had been like a revelation of different levels of thought, but the Laws that God said would be revealed were not coming as a list from God. Somehow God was bringing the lessons without revealing his presence. He knew ***they must come from God, and the only way this could be was if, as Renni Nam had said, God was within each of them.***

When the urge to withdraw to the hillside came upon him, which was now impossible, Namuh sought out the company and counsel of Gnieb, (pronounced Nieb). Gnieb was a quiet Nam, the one among all those who had come to the house that resembled Namuh the most. Nothing seemed to disturb him. There was a presence about Gnieb that said to all, *I know who I am and what I am, and I am at peace with this knowledge.*

It wasn't that Gnieb thought himself above the rest or that he felt he was self-sufficient. He simply seemed to glow as an individual and lent strength to all who came to him for advice or help. Namuh welcomed his advice and occasionally became involved in extended conversations about the growing list of Laws that he felt were being revealed to him in the house. On occasion, Gnieb would bring new thoughts to questions that Namuh was pondering.

On this occasion, Namuh said, "Gnieb, I wish that I had come to know you better before the storm. I think we would have become great friends and would have been of help to each other. I wish you had joined me sometimes on my walks on the hillside." Gnieb said, "There is a time and place for everything. If I had known you then, we might very well have caused ourselves a great deal of trouble. You might never have come to the understanding that you gained by your lonely contemplation."

He went on to say, "The time was not right. It is easy to see things now that we would not allow ourselves to even think, much less say to anyone. It is easy now to forget how restricted we were by the Crew Elders and what had become the norm in Nam society. I understood what the Crew Elders meant when they taught that the Law of the Log required that the Nam see themselves as one, but I never believed we should collapse our individual selves into a mindless cell of this whole. *I can see that we are part of a greater whole but we cannot be a complete whole if, in our own being, we cannot see that we are whole.*"

Namuh stated his thoughts in a question. *"Everything really begins with recognizing our existence as an individual being, doesn't it? I mean there is more to us than a living unit and a part of all living beings, which make up the whole. This being we call ourselves is like a part of God. This is what really gives us being. All power to do and be comes from inside us. At the core of what I think of as Namuh is the being that sustains this life force. It is this being that emanates thought. Thought, along with emotion, is creative, and the power of this thought originates in the being."*

Gnieb said, "I knew you had found Renni Nam. I recognized this new strength in you after the trial and in the manner in which you asked for help with building the house. I knew that something extraordinary had happened in the Council when you were called by the Crew Elders to answer for your actions.

I thought of this as a problem you would have to work out alone, but I should have come to help you. I have been too self-sufficient, even a little conceited in what I thought of as knowledge of Self. I had adopted the attitude that it would do no good and only cause myself problems to speak my mind. I thought of myself as the only one who recognized that this being within is all important to understand."

"Even when you began to build the house, I did not come to help. I watched the daily work from a distance. I said to myself that Namuh will bring forth great ideas and accomplish great things. It was the being within you pushing outward that attracted me. I was preparing to approach you as the storm broke. In fact, I was on the way here when it began. That is why I was one of the first to arrive. You are right, the beginning and the end are in the inner being."

CHAPTER TWENTY-ONE

ACTION

The house was filling up with Nam, and the Wonk was providing sustenance, but the pressure for space increased, and time was getting short for those still outside exposed to the elements. Namuh knew that the single efforts of those who traveled outward were not enough. His thoughts turned to how to save those who were too numbed by the cold to save themselves. They had to become aware that a way and a place existed for them.

They knew the house existed, but he knew there were many who could not get to the surface. They were buried in the snow, and even if they could get to the surface they could see little in the gale that seemed to never let up. It was all but impossible to go to them, but he had to find a way to let them know that they could come to the house.

Maybe they simply did not believe they could get to it, and if they could, maybe they did not believe it could save them. *Maybe "belief" had something to do with God's Laws. They had to know the house was available, but did they believe they could get to it and be welcomed?* In any event, the remaining Nam would have to do the same as those who had come. The house was there *but it would have to be by their own actions that salvation was found.* They would have to be the instrument of their own salvation because Namuh's teams could not force them to come.

Everyday he climbed up further than any of the others had settled; levels above all the den. He was trying to assimilate what he was learning. He was thinking about the experiences that were being reported and what he was coming to recognize as *irrefutable and unchangeable Laws*. He did not understand everything he observed, but there was a pattern, and those he recognized seemed to fit with one another. He seldom spoke, but he listened intently.

He was cheered by the stories the teams reported about their searches for possible survivors. Eveileb (Eve) and Wonk, as had many in the house, continually risked their lives in attempts to find relatives. Often they could find no one or even the house as the village and farmhouses were completely buried in snow. The wind seemed never to abate.

The searchers themselves ran the risk of being unable to make it back to the house where they knew food and shelter awaited. Those who survived the longest were those who were buried in the houses and thus were protected from the weather. Those exposed to the elements did not last long. Some had, by accident or by intent, not taken the allotted food to the animal shelters. Some had gone to their animal shelters surviving off of animal flesh or the Wonk they had allotted for the animals.

Eve and Wonk had found Eve's sister. They thought that they had been lucky because if her sister's husband had not come up from the house through the tunnel he had dug, they would never have found them. They had literally stumbled into him. He had taken them to what had been the animal shelter for the family. They were an awful sight; dirty, starving and literally freezing.

They had already killed, and long since consumed, the last of the stock. There was not enough fuel to keep the water from freezing. No sooner would they melt snow for water than it would begin to freeze. They were so numbed by the cold that they appeared to have difficulty thinking clearly, though they knew Eve and Wonk.

At first they would not hear of leaving even when Eve described the house and the salvation they had found. Her brother-in-law began to moan about the punishment that Pilot had brought upon them. If they further defied Pilot by going to the house of Missile, there was no telling what Pilot would do.

After some hours of ineffective argument, Eve finally cried from pure frustration. Her tears seemed to move her sister as if a long forgotten memory cord had been rung. She rushed as best she could to her side and Eve embraced her. Eve was desperate and began to shake her. "You must believe that if you come to the house you and your family can live. If Pilot were going to do anything, he would not have allowed us to find you. Stop and think. Make yourself think. If we have found shelter and food and want to share it with you, it must be out there. How else could we be here?"

"You KNOW this is true. It is not a matter of faith only. We are here. We have come to take you to safety. You need only believe this and prepare for the trip. We are with you. We will help with the children." Eve's sister had turned to her husband and said, "My sister would not have come if the house was not still there and with an abundance of food. See. They are strong and healthy." Eve said, "The only thing keeping you from the safety of the house and all the food you can eat is your own lack of belief. If you can only muster the belief and the will to try, we will help you get there."

Eve's sister and family had made it safely to the house that Namuh had built and had soon become a productive unit in the group. Namuh had marveled at the fine line between knowing and believing. The stress had always been on faith, the belief that Pilot was all-powerful and would provide everything they needed. The Crew Elders had taught at length about believing, but Namuh could see from the experience related by Eve and Wonk that *belief alone was not enough. Knowledge alone was not enough. With all the knowledge in the world and no faith, nothing of consequence would happen. With nothing but pure blind faith, things could happen, but without knowledge first, this faith could easily be misplaced.*

CHAPTER TWENTY-TWO

PURE POTENTIALITY

After a planning session with the objective of finding and mobilizing others still outside the house, it was decided to focus on leaders in the Nam community. The idea was to help find all those who might be a positive influence on the rest of the community. All those who were living and could be found, if influenced by these leaders to save themselves, would come to the house. One massive effort before it was too late was deemed necessary now, without further delay.

Erup Laitnetop was chosen as the captain of this rescue mission. Erup had proven himself strong-willed and a man with great energy. He was also very thoughtful and determined. Those who would accompany him would be Namuh, Amrak and Evlove. Amrak was the only Crew Elder who had sought the sanctuary of the house. His testimony was all they had that might carry weight with other Crew Elders.

This rescue team went in search of the house of Worran. It was felt that if they could help the old man, maybe he could convince the Crew Elders that Pilot had provided the house for their salvation. Maybe then, they would not consider going to the house to be a form of rebellion against Pilot. If Worran would come, it would show that those who had gone to the house were not rebellious against the Crew Elders but were simply taking the only logical step to save themselves and their fellow Nam.

No tunnels had been dug from Worran's house, and because it sat alone in an open area, there were no exact landmarks to guide them. It was bitterly cold, and the wind and snow made the task even more difficult. A line tied to their waists connected the four.

Erup was determined to find Worran though both Amrak and Evlove eventually had urged the abandonment of the effort before they put themselves in peril. The team happened upon the site only because the wolves had been digging in the snow trying to get into the house and because of the location of the depression made it noticeable.

The wolves were starving too or they would not have ventured from the protection of their dens. They had not, however, been able to get into the house. Worran was frozen in sleep, and there was nothing they could do. Amrak noted, "Raef and Regna's house is located exactly 81 paces south of here. I know because I paced it off when I helped with the stones for Worran's property wall. It intersects with Raef's eastern wall. While we are here, we should see if there is anything we can do for them."

While the smoke was not visible in the storm, when they approached the spot where the 81 paces took them, the airshaft was visible above the snow. They had walked almost upon it. They began to dig where they thought the door would be. The snow was not hard packed, and they soon came to the wall of the house. Clearing space along it until they reached the door, they began pounding on it.

Sounds inside were a long time coming, but eventually Regna assisted with opening the door. She was worn and gray, obviously weakened by the cold and hunger, but no less the stormy personality she had always been. She demanded to know why they were there. The house that Namuh built was the work of Missile, and they were his henchmen. Had they come to taunt them?

Evlove assured her that they had come only out of concern for their well-being and safety. Regna demanded to know if they had brought food or fuel. Evlove explained that it was difficult to come at all and that their purpose was to help them escape the storm to the house Namuh had built. Regna began to rage again that the house was the work of Missile and that she and Raef remained faithful to to the Great God Pilot.

99

Raef appeared from the back room looking even more haggard than Regna. He had lost none of his brooding appearance, though he seemed quiet and fearful as if their presence represented some danger. The visitors were offered no hot drink or even the courtesy of a chair. Their fuel was almost gone, and the team had expected no great courtesy from Raef and Regna anyway. Namuh had determined to let Evlove and Erup do the talking. He felt anything he might say would be counter-productive. Evlove began by relating events at the house.

She told how those who had come to the house represented a broad cross section of the Nam population. There was no strange god in the house, much less Missile. These were the common members of the Nam society who had gathered together for safety. They worked together with common purpose. They were thankful that the Crew Elders had allowed Namuh to build the house and store the excess Wonk as the house and the Wonk had been their salvation. In fact, it had been the farsightedness of the Crew Elders in allowing this that so many had been saved.

Instead of grasping this olive leaf offered by Evlove, Raef reacted angrily. He said, "It was Worran alone who had allowed the building of the house, and it was not my decision to allow the excess Wonk to be taken there. I know the house is the work of Missile, and I have remained loyal to Pilot. He has brought this great punishment upon us, and we must endure it or die."

Amrak, in a stroke of insight spoke up. He said, "Raef, can you not see that this one idea, whether it came from Namuh's imaginings, from Pilot or even Missile, has meant the salvation of the Nam people? How do you know Pilot did not provide this idea to Namuh?" Raef simply said, "That is not possible. He would have communicated with Worran or me."

Erup said, "We have found few survivors outside the house. Those we have found are almost out of fuel and have little or no food. Aside from those in the house, there may be no survivors if this storm lasts another week or even a few days more."

Again Amrak spoke, "Think about it. This one idea, regardless of its origin, has saved many. It has taught us how to store enough to withstand the harshest winter. By building such houses all over the valley, there will always be shelter and food. Think about the power of this one simple idea to save a whole people. Think what it will mean for future generations of Nam." Raef answered, "It is better that every Nam die to the last man, woman and child than to succumb to the works of Missile and his servant Namuh."

"Namuh is the Anti-Pilot." Raef glared at Namuh and appeared almost the Raef of old. "We were warned that someone among the people would come representing Missile. We thought we had banished the servant of Missile when we exiled Renni Nam. I never thought I would hear a Crew Elder saying such things. Missile has won, but as for me and the other Crew Elders, we will never bow down to the Anti-Pilot."

There was no use for further discussion. *When the mind is closed, it cannot receive,* thought Namuh. The three turned away and climbed back to the surface, beginning the trek back to the house, sinking deeply into the snow. Pulling and pushing each other against the wind, they trudged along. It was useless to talk, and they were all occupied with their own thoughts.

Namuh would not have put it the way Amrak, Evlove and Erup had, but what they had said was probably the best approach. It had not worked, but he doubted that Raef would have accepted anything they could have said.

One thing Amrak had said struck a cord with Namuh. He had not thought about the construction of the house in that way, but it was true. *The single idea to build the house had meant the salvation of many. Everything had begun with this idea. Other ideas such as storing Wonk in the house had come, attracted to the first. From this came the natural progression as a shelter in the storm. The house then became the center for organizing the salvation of many Nam. Yes, thoughts were powerful.*

101

Later when they were safe in the house, he could not get his mind off of this thought. *Everything begins with thought. Thought is pure potentiality. Without thought, nothing could exist. He stated it again in a different way. "Everything that existed had first existed in thought."*

He continued to dwell on the idea. *If the thought was good, it created constructively. In other words, if the thought was good, good was created, and if the thought was bad, it still created. What a bad thought did, however, was create destructively*. For instance, Raef's thinking about Pilot also created, but it had created destruction. It was destroying a large portion of the Nam people. This too must be one of the Universal Laws that he had been told would be revealed in the house. *Thought has the pure potential for the creation of constructive or destructive results*.

Namuh now frequented a level of the house no one else even visited. He must think. This whole plan, the house and the needs of the people had caused him to think in a different way. Sometimes he just seemed to know what others were thinking. Sometimes he thought, and it seemed like God, Renni Nam or somebody else was inside his head, and they were both thinking the same thoughts at the same time.

Namuh, reliving his experiences, waxed back and forth between positive thoughts and negative, fearful doubts. Maybe it was just luck. Maybe it was God. Maybe it was Missile. He scolded himself, "Now you have to think. You have to find a way to help the lost Nam, and later you can think about where the benefits you have experienced have come from.

If only we had built more houses for God, if only we had saved more Wonk. That's it! This thought had come before, but now it was clear. God had given him the seed of an idea when He had told him to build Him a house. We can build houses like this all over the valley. We can have enough to support the search for ways through the mountains. Here in the valley, no Wonk will be lost! We can plant more, and there will be more space. There is a way! All we have to do is organize so we can make it until the spring.   *The idea had come through understanding of their experiences, but to get the results we want, we must act.*

Namuh's mind now returned to his earlier contemplation of the power of thought. *Everything that could be seen had to have existed first in thought because thought creates form.* It was truly a great thought. This had to be one of the Universal Laws because it was so powerful. *All of the power of God could be accessed by the Nam because there was pure potentiality in thought.   If one believed in his thoughts, it would lead to Action!*

CHAPTER TWENTY-THREE

GIVING

Evig was one of the Nam who had been quick to volunteer to help find those who still had not come to the house. She marveled that it **seemed the more they took in, and the more they gave, the more they seemed to receive**. She said it was now clear to her that they must give if they hoped to receive anything. Namuh had, in his own way, expressed this in his speech to those who had come to the house. At the time, he had not thought of it as a Law, but now understood this principal to be a Law that came from a greater power. Renni Nam, too, had talked about the necessity of giving if one hoped to receive.

It seemed to Namuh that the obvious result of giving provides a multiple return. Evig was voicing questions that were in Namuh's mind as well. She wondered why this was not evident to everyone. She said, "We simply get so involved in our own needs and desires that we can't see that it is in our own interest to give. **Giving of ourselves is the act that produces the results we want for Self.**"

Fles Tseretni, another of the volunteers, said, "When I came to the house, I was only thinking of saving my family. Later I came to understand that **while self-interest was important, only a person blind to the fact that helping others was in his own interest could be so foolish as to be selfish. How could a man think that his own interest could be served without assisting others? There is little one can do for one unwilling to accept assistance or incapable of receiving help, but one's self-interest is best served by helping those who need help.**"

Fles had been one of the last survivors to bring his family to the house, but he had spoken of others in his family he had to find. It was as if this had not occurred to him until he and his family had made it to the house. He said that when he had decided to come to the house, he had given little thought of his brother except to hope he too was on the way to the house. "I was not physically fit to find him as I barely made it to the house, but as soon as I was able, this became my overriding objective."

Namuh noted something he said that had sounded almost like the words of Renni Nam. Fles had said, *"You can't help someone else if you are unable to help yourself, but then you can't help yourself without helping others."* He had chosen to come to the house, and when his strength had returned, with the help of others in the house, they had found his brother.

When they had found Fles' brother, he at first had been unwilling to be helped. He had no capacity to be helped. He couldn't grasp the fact that there was a large body of Nam living in a house a short distance from him, warm and comfortable, with plenty to eat. No one in the village had the strength now to go anywhere, yet his brother Fles and his companions were strong. They could have come only if they had had food and shelter.

Once he agreed to come and fully understood that there was safety at hand, he had asked Fles why he had not come for him before. Fles said, "I too refused to go to the house until I was almost too weak to make it. If it had not been for those who found me, I would have died. If I had persisted in my refusal of help, I would certainly have died. Fles said, **"My desire to save my family was great, but I had taken no steps to accomplish this objective. It took both those willing to help and my willingness to help myself."**

Namuh had thought about this phenomena before. *He knew that the first obligation was to fulfill one's purpose*. Under no circumstance could others be allowed to divert him from his purpose. *He had to be capable of helping others, and they had to be capable of responding to his help*. It was another principal that Namuh would ponder in the long hours of the night as the wind wailed outside.

Namuh knew that he had grown in stature in the eyes of the Nam people, and this was primarily due to his giving of what he was capable of giving. After all the derision, they recognized the house to be his idea. What they had considered silly was now the symbol of Pilot to them. It seemed to Namuh that, for the majority of those in the house, Pilot had simply used Namuh as the instrument of their salvation. Now no one questioned the fact that Pilot had talked to Namuh and had bypassed the Crew Elders. Because of Renni Nam's discourse, Namuh knew that *the inner spirit he said had come to him was not the war god Pilot,* but this was not the time to argue the point with those in the house.

He mused to himself, "The next thing I know, some of those who have come will be worshipping the house." Universal Being, or whatever name given to God, was the origin and was responsible. Namuh knew this, but he still felt a little resentment due to the fact that no one had contributed to its construction, and God had not, as far as he could tell for sure, come to the house.

He and his family had carried every stone, pulled each up to the level where he was working. *When he gave as he had over the past year and was continuing to do, the benefits returned were many times the giving.* No doubt he could ask for a tribute and receive such from each who had found safety through him and the house he built. It was not an idea he seriously considered. *He was now the acknowledged leader and knew himself to be one with those who had come to the house.*

Namuh was so grateful for all that God had provided that he was able to look past the fact that no one had helped and that, at one stage, his life had been in the balance. He marveled at the way new ideas and answers came just when he needed something. He felt that the lessons God had promised were being provided in such abundance that he could not carry on his duties and absorb them. He had to find a way to quiet his mind to have the understanding he sought.

Namuh was now sure he did not believe the fearsome stories that the Crew Elders told about the anger and power of God. Pilot might very well have existed, and he might have done all that had been recorded about his visits, but this could not be Universal Being, the creative force in all life. Pilot was not the one who had come to him in his dream. *Pilot was not the Universal Being that Renni Nam had talked about. One thing Namuh was sure of, his contact with God was through his search within himself, not outside in the mountains, at the temple of the Great Bird, nor from the Crew Elders and the Log.*

Even the understanding that he was gaining brought him no peace as the daily struggle wore on. Again he sought the solitude of another level where no Nam came for advice, to cry on his shoulder or demand redress. In the solitude of this level, he thought of all that had happened and all that he had done for the people. Would he have done anything like this if it had not been for the dream?

Even if God had not used the house, it was fortunate that he had built it. "If I had not built it, the people would have perished. At the same time, had I not taken the action that I took, my family and I would have faced the same end. I have given more than the others. I have given everything, but I don't need any return from the Nam people. I will always give and keep on giving but without expectation of return from any single individual. I can expect the return because it simply seems to be a rule. If I want something, I must first give, and when I give, I get much more in return. This has brought us to where we are, and this will see us through."

Namuh noted the facts, *"I have also learned that I must give to all but there are those who cannot receive."* He asked himself, "How does this fit together? *If I want to receive, I must give, but I can only effectively give to those who can receive. When I give something, what am I really giving? What has led to all the giving, and what am I expressing when I give?"*

107

Remembering what Evol had said, he repeated it aloud, ***"It all comes down to love. If I did not love the people of Nam, I would not have gone through the severe trials I have suffered."*** He asked himself, "Who was the major recipient of benefits?" But he already knew the answer. He thought, ***"No matter what I have given, I have received more than I have given. I am the one who has benefited most."***

CHAPTER TWENTY-FOUR

THE AWAKENING

These Laws God had talked about in the dream were now very real to Namuh. *It was not because God had revealed them in the dream like a set of commands, but because Namuh had experienced each and understood them. He also understood that he did not have a complete knowledge. He thought that these Laws must have many levels of understanding for the one who pursued such knowledge. They were not easy but formed what he had come to see as a set of principles that could be described as perfect justice. They were the one absolute truth in the life of Nam. When experienced and understood, it was as if each was somehow felt. It was not a matter of written commands as in the Great Log but were truths from within expressed outwardly.*

These Universal Laws had been here for the Nam all along. Renni Nam had taught some of them. Namuh simply had not understood them because he had been too young to experience them. *They were revealed here in the house because it was here that he experienced them. Was there anything in his dream that was not here manifested in reality? The creation had been in the thought, and the manifestation in the understanding of these great principles.*

Namuh had been conscious of changes within himself, but until he was moved to speak to all the Nam, it had not formed a pattern in his conscious thinking. **Why!** he thought to himself, *it had been like building a house with his mind. Maybe this was the house God had been talking about and not the one he had built with stone and timber.*

He thought back to his concerns in the beginning at the first level of the house. He had been disappointed and personally felt

109

rejected because God had not come to the house. He was not thinking of anyone but himself. When the Nam began to come, once the storm had broken upon them, he had been personally gratified. He felt vindicated with the acknowledgment of the Nam that maybe he had been right after all.

As it had become crowded and he had moved up to the second level, he had been overcome with emotion. It was not as if he had simply been in an emotional state, but that he had been in touch with his emotions. *He was emotionally involved but not emotionally attached or controlled by them. He had become aware that emotion reached through up and down the levels of his thinking and produced different results at each level.*

At the third level, he had become more aware of the Self as distinct from others and even the Nam that he thought of as Namuh. Sometimes he thought he was more in touch with Renni Nam than the Namuh who the people knew. *He was conscious of what he had done, how he was perceived and what role he was to play. But, more importantly, he was conscious of the unfolding Self that was responsible for the Namuh others perceived.*

At the fourth level, he became conscious of the need to work with others. Those who had come to the house had to be made aware of the power they could access and what they could do for those who as yet had not made it to the house. He had felt it before, but it was becoming so pronounced that he was fully aware. He was not afraid! Fear had subsided when he had talked to Renni Nam. In standing before the Crew Elders, he had felt the fear disappear for a while as he became focused on the mission of making them see the fear that lived in their hearts. *Now, fear had slipped away. Beaten, it had retreated from his thoughts.*

At the fifth level, he had become conscious of the power of the mind, the creative power of thought. *Combined with thought was the recognition that by believing in the creative power of his thoughts and surrendering to the outcome, he created materially.* He also gained knowledge. What knowledge was it that was so important? *He thought it was the knowing that what was manifested or became a material reality was already created by the thought. Nothing could be realized without first the creative power of thought.*

At the sixth level, the love for his fellow Nam, even those who had tried to destroy him, had burst from within him like a great power that was forcing or beaming it outwardly. He had no desire for repayment for all that he had done for the people of Nam, nor had he any desire for vengeance. *They were one and the same with him, and their fate had been his. They were all part of the whole.* He was at peace with himself and all Nam. He thought it a blissful state. Certainly he was full of joy.

Before the storm, Namuh had often been a solitary figure. Aside from his family and his work, Namuh had spent a large part of his time alone with his thoughts. Dimit, his childhood friend, had frequently come to the house, but he was unobtrusive and rarely engaged Namuh in discussions other than of a mundane nature. Namuh had made few close friends outside of this small circle.

What he had discovered in the house was that many were expressing thoughts that would have been considered by the Crew Elders to be against the laws of Pilot. Maybe they had thought this way all along but had been afraid to voice these ideas. Maybe even now they did not think of these ideas as anything but good common sense gleaned from the harsh realities of the crisis they had faced. It wasn't as if they were formulating a religion or philosophy. They were simply making observations from their experiences in the house.

Renni Nam had said, *"There is no way to understand the Universal Laws without personal experience of them."* It was true that you could feel the loss of someone who had a father, mother, sister or brother die. You could feel the pain of the mother who had lost a child. *No matter how much sympathy you felt, however, the fact is that you could not know how they felt until you experienced such a loss.*

The inhabitants of the house were expressing in their own ways the truths that they themselves experienced. He had thought of himself as the only one who listened to others and had doubted that anyone else was listening as closely as he to what was being said. *He now knew that he was not alone in recognizing these truths, and he knew that these were the very Laws that he had been told would be revealed to him in the house.*

Namuh knew that knowing the Laws alone was not sufficient. It was only a beginning. At least, if one knew the Laws; one knew something of Universal Being. He thought, "Each of these Laws is like a revelation of the nature of Universal Being. Each is an expression of truth, a divine expression of God. With time, one could learn more and more about the purposes of Universal Being and about one's own purpose. These truths were like lights pointing the way to even deeper meaning that one could understand through experience. Life was about learning, and Laws were the basis from which all learning sprang.

CHAPTER TWENTY-FIVE

NAMUH SPEAKS

There seemed no end to the wind, ice and bitter cold. Namuh was cheered by the smooth running of his organization that daily brought more to the House, including salvaged supplies. It was no longer a bunch of survivors huddling against the elements. It was a dedicated group with a purpose. However, he still had concerns.

There had never been such a sustained storm, and it was becoming more and more difficult to recover supplies. While he had come to have some understanding of the Laws, including The Law of Abundance, years of dealing with winter shortages had conditioned him to be fearful. He was afraid that regardless of their successes, in the end, there would not be enough. The question in Namuh's mind was, could they last until spring?

In his inner thoughts, he knew there was meaning to what had happened. Would God give him this blessing and help him save the Nam people and then allow all to die when the Wonk ran out? This was simply something he could not believe. He understood that *what had been conceived and believed had been achieved. What had worked would continue to work.* There was no doubt in his mind that this was one of the Laws God had said would be revealed in the house.

He thought of all he had learned from this frightful experience. He numbered the truths he had come to understand. Many Laws he had come to understand because of those who worked in his teams. He had discussed them with each who had expressed them, adding to his own storehouse of knowledge and understanding. He thought, *"Now is the time to share my understanding with all who have come to the house. The more I share, the more I give, the more I receive. If I want greater understanding, I will have to give of the understanding that I have!"*

He prayed that he would be given the proper words to communicate with the people of Nam, these survivors of the worst storm in memory. It would not be easy for him to put into words what he had come to know and wanted to share. There was no way to know what their reaction would be, but the time had come.

He called a meeting of the community that shared the house. They gathered from the ground level to the sixth level. They sat on the stairs and around the shaft so that all could hear. Many thought that Namuh would announce the cessation of the winds, but they could still hear the roar outside. All knew that this was a meeting of great import because Namuh had never called such a meeting. He had not presumed to teach. He seemed to keep his own council and had only spoken to the group when it was still small and when the need to help those still outside the protection of the house had moved him to do so.

He stood for a long while at the entrance to the roof until everyone had found a place and the noise from so many in a confined area had completely ceased. Still he stood as if uncertain what to say. He began to speak slowly but loud enough to be heard above the noise of the storm which itself had lessened.

"You are all my brothers and sisters. We are all Nam", he said. "We have worked together and lived together as one family. We have shared all that we have. Those of you who have worked on the teams going outside, as well as those of you who have worked inside to make our survival possible, have shared with me your thoughts and this has greatly benefited me. At one time, I thought that I had given the most but now I see that I, as has been my nature, have not shared all with you. In fact, I have not shared my thinking and the Laws that God has revealed in this house."

"What I am about to reveal to you is not a new set of Laws such as you were familiar with and were taught by the Crew

114

Elders.   Rather, *these Laws are principles and truths upon which I have come to understand that all Laws, even the physical laws of nature, are based.   These Laws have been present for all Nam from the beginning of time. They have always been available for us, but we have only been impressed by the exercise of power and controlled by fear.*

I no longer believe that the laws as revealed by the Crew Elders are the Laws of Universal Being or what we call God. The laws of Pilot were interpreted by the Crew Elders. However, it is apparent to me that Pilot was an alien being in our midst. He revealed his laws to the Crew Elders, but they were laws given to him and were not meant for the Nam people. Even these laws are perversions of the Universal Laws of God. Pilot was a powerful being in that he could easily kill and had developed a technology that even today we do not understand.

I do not believe that the original intent of the Crew Elders was to mislead us, but they lacked understanding of what Pilot's laws actually were. As time went on, new ideas about these laws lead to the creation of more laws, many of which were designed to maintain control. In the past years leading up to this terrible storm, there were Crew Elders who attempted to maintain their control by fear and by keeping us ignorant.

The Universal Laws of which I now speak are not based upon stories or beliefs in written commands. I do not propose that these Laws, which I will reveal to you today, must be believed. It is not a matter of blind faith but a matter of knowing. When one understands these Laws — one <u>knows</u>. When one knows, then one gains the faith that because these Laws exist, what we create in thought will be manifested in reality. I am simply revealing to you the Laws as I have come to understand them, many of which I came to understand when you experienced them first and then revealed your experiences to me.

I am not proposing a new religion nor will I be your Navigator. Each Nam must take responsibility for himself.

Each must discover for himself if he is to gain understanding of these Laws. I am sharing my understanding, and you can use this understanding for your benefit. You may choose to leave this house in the spring and again create whatever way of life you want. You can even find among yourselves those who are prepared to be Crew Elders and continue to follow the Law of the Log. You can continue to live in Love or you can again live in fear. What you think, you will create. What you think, you will become. Your life is your creation.

My understanding of the Laws revealed in this house I have categorized into thirteen. This does not mean that there can't be more or less, but this is how I have come to understand them. In time, there may be those who will develop a better understanding of these Laws and even greater benefits may be discovered. Certainly God is not limited. I have come to understand that these 13 Laws are actually the Divine Self-Expression. By this I mean all thirteen are expressions of the nature of God.

This Universal Being is beyond our comprehension but it is in all physical beings. We can know something of it only by knowing Self. I cannot fathom the whole of God, but I can reveal some of the principles which make up this unchanging Being. I cannot reveal to you everything about God, but I can identify those who have claimed to be God, but who are not God, by understanding of the Universal Laws, which are the Divine Expression of God.

We can understand these principles on some level. It may not be deep or complete, but these Laws have always been available to us. I believe we have always recognized these principles on a very basic level but simply have never conceived of them as universal principles. I present to you only my understanding, but simply believing what I say will not be enough. Memorizing what I say will not be sufficient. I know that you are grateful to me for the help I have rendered to you, but you will do yourselves a disservice to follow what I say blindly. I ask you only to think about the Universal Laws, the

Laws of Life as I have come to understand them, and delve into your own experiences for understanding of how these principles have applied in your life.

CHAPTER TWENTY-SIX

THE UNIVERSAL LAWS

1)   There is great power in the individual. If one Nam, simply by having a strange dream, can provide the salvation for all the people in the valley who would come, there is tremendous power in each person. The individual is the important unit of the whole. The single being is the source of all, and there is more to this being than just a body to work in the fields. It was my expression of what God wanted that has saved the Nam. This principle I call THE LAW OF BEING.

2)   At the same time, I am part of the whole of the Nam. We are all different but interdependent. We must have Wonk and the animals must have it too. We must have the animals to survive, and they must have Wonk and us. Everything is connected. The real world is diverse but no matter how great the diversity, there is still unity. One becomes the many, and sameness becomes variety and diversity. There is one life expressing itself in many ways. All is contained within the whole of being. This is THE LAW OF ABSOLUTE UNITY.

3)   What if my view or perspective had been the same as the Crew Elders? I, along with all those who came to the house, would be dead. There would no longer be the people of Nam. Maybe even my perspective is wrong. Maybe I did not quite get the point of the dream where God demanded I build the house. Maybe the house was never for anyone but the Nam. Maybe by building the house and providing a safe haven for the Nam, this house is for God.

*This too is one of God's Universal Laws, **THE LAW OF PROPER PERSPECTIVE.***

4) *My thoughts, whether fully understood or not, have been the instrument of Nam salvation. Consciousness, Intelligence or Mind is the most fundamental thing in and of the Universe and, therefore, is the essential substance of our inner being. The power of thought allowed me to continue the creation process of the Nam. All of us are creating our lives daily. It is our living masterpiece. This is the indestructible part of Nam.*

All things in existence first exist in thought, and without thought, there can be no form. What is conceived in thought can take form. A thought, therefore, creates form. If a thing cannot be thought, it cannot exist. This fact alone proves beyond any doubt the existence of the thinker. It proves the existence of Universal Being — the God Renni Nam spoke of.

The creative principle of the universe is not an accident. It is specific in principle like the natural law of gravity. There is nothing capricious or changeable about its operation. It cannot be deceived into imparting its benefits to us. I concentrated on what I saw as necessary. I focused with undivided attention on my objective, and using visualization, I clearly determined and designed the desired outcome. This is one of the Universal Laws God said would be revealed in the house and that each of us possesses — THE LAW OF PURE POTENTIALITY.

5) *What if I had not been convinced of the reality of the dream? I knew and, therefore, believed. My belief overcame my doubts and fears. Based upon this belief, I acted. What if I had not done so? What if my family had not believed in me? Could I have finished the house?*

119

What if no one had believed and come to the house? In order to use the almighty power of the Universal Laws, I had to actually put myself in the hands of the almighty power of these Universal Principles. I placed myself in the hands of God. I call this THE LAW OF BELIEVING AND KNOWING.

6) *I know that the natural order of the universe is abundance. This is not a world of need and shortages. Our minds, our thinking, have created negative conditions just as readily as favorable ones, and it is through negative thinking that we created shortages in our lives. Because of our thinking, we could not break the cycle of winter hardship. This Law, like the other Universal Laws, is in constant operation and is relentless. It brings exactly what is created in thought. This is THE LAW OF ABUNDANCE.*

7) *When we are in harmony with Universal Laws and understand their operation, we are sending out currents charged with power. What we have attracted has little to do with what we hope to have or wish we had. It is very important that we think constructive thoughts, because what we think is what we become. All the really good things of life have been brought to me beginning with the maintenance of life itself. This is THE LAW OF ATTRACTION.*

8) *Underlying the different levels of creation and all life in the valley is a substance that remains integrated in its value, even when on the surface, it continues to give rise to qualities of an ever changing nature. This experience has revealed for me the process in nature and shows the relation of all to all. Everything in the valley and the universe God talked about is constantly influencing every other thing. All relate to each other, and there is correspondence between all planes of life. In everything,*

there is substance, motion and awareness. This connection of all to all I call THE LAW OF RELATIVITY.

9) *Everywhere I see harmony and balance in all things. In this valley, as I suspect is the case in every valley, nature constantly seeks to rectify any imbalance and express harmony in all things. In the smallest bit of life to the largest, there is balance. There are no exceptions to this or any of these Laws. I have attempted to put myself in accordance with the natural flow of nature, though that may sometimes appear to be impossible. I understand, when it comes to balance, nature makes no mistakes. The universe without and within simply makes adjustments, which are all about equalization and balance. We as individual beings, and the Nam as a whole, must have balance in our lives, in our perspectives and in our thinking. God's balance and equalization is the perfect justice that we find impossible to create here in the valley and in our dealings with others. This I call THE LAW OF BALANCE AND EQUALIZATION.*

10) *We have slowly grown in understanding. Our thinking and our blind adherence to the Law of the Log had blocked this growth. Our understanding of our being was not allowed to unfold. Everything in our lives has been slowly changing, evolving in time due to our constant striving within the matter of which we are made. The situation in which we have found ourselves has accelerated the process. This is THE LAW OF EVOLUTION AND UNFOLDMENT.*

11) *Of what benefit would it have been had I not shared the house and the Wonk with all of you? We would still be in the old cycle of destruction, limited in the old ways, without knowledge of or belief in ourselves. What good would it have been to survive alone here in the valley? My giving*

has caused all to give, and the giving has brought great benefits to the whole of Nam. What else could I have done? What other action could I possibly have taken that would not have ended in the death of all including myself and my family? Giving was my only course of non-destructive action. This too is one of the Universal Laws, THE LAW OF GIVING.

12) *In order to receive the benefits that the surviving Nam have brought, I had to give. It is clear to me that this is a Universal Law. It is natural that one can give only what one is capable of giving and can only receive what one is capable of receiving. I was in the position to give. By doing so, I was in a position to receive. Without the giving, I could not have received. It was, therefore, in my self-interest to give. This is THE LAW OF RIGHTEOUS SELF-INTEREST.*

13) *Love is an in-flowing and out-flowing, giving and receiving, with complete understanding. When I, and later the Nam in the house, gave to others, what did we give? It was not just Wonk and shelter in the house. It was expressed that way, but it was more than food and shelter. It was life itself. Love corresponds in the physical laws of nature as the life force. It is the love of life that drives animals, plants and all life to survive. Knowing The Law of Giving, I have come to understand that whether we give food, shelter or knowledge, all we are really giving is Love. All that we can give is Love. This is THE LAW OF LOVE.*

There they are in my own experience, the Laws God promised would be revealed in the house. They were revealed not by a voice but by life itself. Everything I was told in the dream has happened. It was not as I had imagined in my ignorance but as I have experienced in the light of living and understanding. Now I have shared this understanding, and this act itself is The Law of Giving."

When Namuh finished speaking, there was silence. Each mind was filled with memories that corresponded to the Laws of which Namuh had spoken. It was not a matter of each understanding the whole of what he had said but that each knew from their experience that what he said was true. Each was thinking of his own understanding of one or more of the Laws.

Suddenly, all were talking, asking questions and telling their friends about some experience that showed their understanding or lack of complete understanding of a Law. There was great excitement among the Nam people because they understood that these were Laws that had always existed for them. All they had to do was apply what they had heard from Namuh to see for themselves whether what he said was true or not. The proof would come from their lives and experiences. With understanding, they would know the truth, and the truth would make them free.

CHAPTER TWENTY-SEVEN

NAMUH'S HOUSE

Now as Namuh looked out from the top of the house, the seventh and final level, he realized Renni Nam was with him. Had he somehow made it through all the obstacles of the storm, or had he been with him all along? Namuh thought there had been many times when Renni Nam had seemed close. Maybe it had been Renni Nam who had spoken to him on those occasions when he had heard the voice.

Namuh had never been to the top of the house except during construction. None of those who helped move the Wonk had been there. Those who had glimpsed the top from the sixth level were fearful of the height and were afraid to go up. Even Namuh and his family had been careful not to look from the top during construction. They were unaccustomed to such heights, and it was too much like playing at being God. They had averted their eyes from the view because if they inadvertently caught glimpses that attracted their attention, they felt lightheaded.

Today, he had at last gone to the top of the house because the winds had died and sunlight was visible. Spring had to be coming soon or at least the storm must be over. Namuh was thankful because their stock of Wonk had been largely consumed. *He knew there was abundance as there had always been plenty. He had learned that this was one of the Laws. Somehow, from somewhere, they had attracted what they needed.*

He reviewed the situation as he stood, along with Renni Nam, at the top. He was not alone, nor for the first time did he feel alone. Sometimes even with a house full of Nam, he had felt the great burden of his responsibility and had felt as if he alone carried it. *Now he truly felt as one with the people of*

124

Nam and all life that had been sleeping with the winter. Life was springing out all over, and he was further emboldened by the presence of Renni Nam who still had said nothing about how he came to be there.

There was no Big Bird, but from the top he could see far into the ranges in all directions. Clearly this was seeing with eyes that had not seen before. Renni Nam had shown him there was access to the outside from near his hut. There had to be other passes that led through the mountains, and if one faced the task of finding and charting them, they would be available for all.

His experience of the climb to find Renni Nam's valley in the mountain had convinced him there were mysteries there that no one had imagined. The Nam could themselves find the valley with no winters, *but now there was no reason to escape. They knew how to protect themselves from the harsh winters. They knew how to survive the worst of storms in comfort and with plenty of Wonk.*

There must be people in the other valleys like the Valley of Nam! They could come here, and we could go to their valleys. There must be things that the Nam could produce, like Wonk that these people would like to have. There would be things that Nam could bring back to the valley that would make their lives easier. The world was not all rock, and it was not just a sea of never ending ice and snow.

On the roof of the house, the sun was bright. He already felt that he was in a light brighter than the sun. *He knew there was much more to know, but this experience had been necessary to his unfoldment. He knew he was one with Universal Being and Renni Nam.* Renni Nam had known and was one with Universal Being. Namuh now knew this to be true. They would, like on the hillside the night of his dream, be in the light and part of this light forever. It was not that they were exclusive and that all Nam were not part of this unity, but they had become aware of the oneness. *Each Nam could come to this awareness.*

Namuh felt the presence of love, power and, yes, this great light. God had been here all the time. *The house that he had built was not only the house of stone and timber that had proved to be the salvation of the Nam, it was also the structure in his mind that he had discovered through the understanding of the Universal Laws. This house of Namuh's inner mind had been further strengthened by the sharing of higher thought and understanding with the people of Nam.*

There was a future for the Nam. From disaster there were now even greater achievements possible. From survival that had seemed in the balance, there was a new hope. The surviving Nam had the beginning of understanding of the Universal Laws, gained from their experiences in the house. With this growing understanding, they would create a new Valley of the Nam. Namuh was reminded of his mother's saying that "It is always darkest before the dawn", and Renni Nam had said, "In every failure was the seed for greater achievement."

Namuh had seen no great bird, nor had God come to him in any form but from his own inner Being. He thought of those who had followed him up the floors, level after level. He understood what it all meant. *It was not a matter of believing rules but of knowing truth. He knew the secrets and understood each level. God had told him the truth would make him free. He was free, and he was not afraid. He knew now that freedom from fear was the greatest freedom and greatest truth of all.*

As he looked out upon the valley, he saw the light shining so brightly it was as if the sun was close to the roof just above the house. The sky was a clear blue, and everywhere there was light. He heard the words without sound. They were clear. *"I've been here all the time, Namuh, in YOUR HOUSE."*

AUTHOR'S NOTE

I am convinced that with even limited knowledge of the Universal Laws, a better understanding of the nature, or attributes of God, is available to us. It is at this point that we can begin the work on Self, and surely we know that there is much work to be done. We should know that the work of humankind must begin with our individual Selves.

I have been a student of the Bible all of my life. I am still a student of the Bible, though I have long since ceased to think of it as the only source of wisdom for man. I think it is evident that the real source is within man himself. This truth too is revealed in the bible. Because of my exposure to religions worldwide, I may have a different perspective from those who have not had the opportunity to live in so many places, but I do not think that it is necessarily an advantage over any person who assumes an open and contemplative attitude.

A study of the religions of the world does not mean that one will necessarily gain a better or more complete understanding of God. There is a great deal of doctrine and dogma mixed in with Universal Truths. I do know that due to my studies of Universal Law, I have come to an understanding that surpasses anything I have learned from any religious dogma. It has caused me to study and compare what the Great Masters have said as opposed to dogma created by those instrumental in building the organizations that were built around these luminaries.

Regardless of the religious tradition we are raised in, to get to the heart of the truth, we must go back to the principles that the Great Masters were teaching in their "simple lessons". Even Jesus' disciples asked him why he taught in the manner that he did. He essentially told them that while they have had the benefit of his personal revelation of the mysteries, his lessons to the people are delivered at the level of their understanding. In

127

other words, the Universal Truths are no less there in each lesson, but you can only give what one is capable of receiving.

It is inconceivable to me that one such as Jesus would spend his life telling stories to entertain the people. There was a great truth, a Universal Law, revealed in each parable. However, these great principles, I suggest, have been relegated to a lower level of importance to that of the apostolic tradition of the death, burial and resurrection of Jesus. Far more importance is given to the doctrines created by the epistles of Paul than to the truths as revealed by Jesus.

The Great Masters did not build religious organizations. These religious disciplines came from those who followed the Great Masters, and I believe it is apparent that their knowledge and evolvement were not of the same standard as the Great Masters. The building of such organizations have served a purpose, but that purpose has not been to reveal the power within man but rather to subvert man to the control of the organization. If we are to be free, Jesus said we would have to know the truth, and the truth would give us this freedom.

Yahweh, the God of Abraham, Jacob and Moses, is described as one with very human characteristics. He had body parts like a man. It is said God became angry, a very human emotion, that he repented having made man, a mistake of un-god-like proportions. He was even made out to be a murderer and as one who incites to murder. Frequent stories of the destruction of a whole people can be found including women and children. Yahweh, the Hebrew God, was described as a being that hungered after the love and affection of his creation yet appeared to be incapable, on a sustained basis, of attracting that love. He showed great favoritism toward a particular bloodline, yet he is supposed to be the creator of all men.

My point is that these descriptions bare no resemblance and are at odds with the descriptions of God as revealed by Jesus and the Great Masters. Those ancient records that reveal events where human characteristics are observed in an entity and that entity is referred to as God, are not Universal Being, the first cause of which the Great Masters spoke.

We know the Universal Laws because the Great Masters revealed them, but they have been covered in the cobwebs of those who followed them and created the religions of the world. Even with all the layers of dogma, the Universal Truths are revealed in world religions and our holy books. The various scriptures we refer to as "Holy" state that God is a spirit, that is, not of physical matter, or not of the same vibratory rate as what we call "physical". We are told that God is omnipotent, that is, all powerful; omnipresent, that is, God is present everywhere; and that God is omniscient, that is, God possesses full knowledge of all knowledge.

The Great Masters have told us that God is the essence of Love, the "all seeing eye", and that His presence is like a blinding light. God is referred to as "The Word" that was before creation in the beginning of time. This is by no means the extent of the descriptions we have from the Great Masters. He is "I Am", the alpha and the omega - the beginning and the end. We are told that His (God's) ways are above our ways and His thoughts above our thoughts as the heavens are higher than the earth. These are hardly human-like characteristics.

How can the human mind comprehend the God the Great Masters spoke of? The fact is, without understanding of The Universal Laws, which are the Divine Self-Expression of God, we cannot comprehend anything remotely close to the essence of Universal Being. We find this impossible because of the doctrines and disciplines developed after the passing of the Great Masters. It is precisely because of the doctrines developed by those who assumed leadership among the surviving followers of the Great Masters that perversions and confusion exist.

Since we find it so difficult to comprehend the nature of God, we humanize Him or we create intermediaries so that we can come to some semblance of comprehension. We do this because we have difficulty in conceiving that God could be within each of us and not an external force or entity in some far off place of majestic proportions. The human need is to understand, but we seem unequipped to understand except in relation to "things" that we do understand, that is, physical "things". We frequently attach ourselves to the one who brings this special wisdom that we consider to be above our wisdom. We are able to understand that a set of laws or principles such as revealed in the parables or beatitudes, ring with a truth or wisdom above ours and, therefore, recognize them as originating with a higher being, but the essence of God eludes us.

My purpose in telling the story of Namuh is not to propagate a new religion. I think we already have more than we need. They serve a purpose at the most basic level of understanding but carry baggage that gets in the way of understanding. I think we have much to learn from the world's major religions, but we must go past doctrines and dogmas to find the Universal Truths taught by the Great Masters. It is important that we do so because the Universal Laws not only reveal how we can benefit from being in harmony with them, but they reveal something of the very nature of God.

The thirteen Universal Laws revealed in the story are all part of The Divine Self - Expression". In other words, they are expressions of Universal Being. Understanding these Universal Truths brings us closer to knowing Self and God.

Regardless of your religious persuasion, and whether or not you believe in a supreme being, the knowledge and benefits of the understanding available through The Universal Laws will surpass any knowledge you may acquire from traditional sources. It is easier to follow dogma, but the benefits and potential for human unfoldment are in experiencing and understanding the Universal Laws. To know God, we must know our Selves, and in the process of coming to know our Selves, we can draw closer to an understanding of Universal Being, for HE IS THERE IN OUR HOUSE.

GLOSSARY OF TERMS

Alpha and Omega - This is another descriptive term for God. It literally means the beginning and the end but represents eternity. It is the circle of eternity, which has no beginning or end.

Amrak - The team member whose experience illustrated the Law of Equalization and Balance.

Anti-Pilot - The designation given to Namuh by Raef. This was the Nam equivalent to the Anti Christ.

Council - The deliberative body of the priest cast. It represents a mind set or body of dogma developed by the priesthood.

Crew Elders - The priestly cast in Nam society. In the story, it is derived from the log left behind by the Captain of the military plane that had come to the valley years before our story.

Dimit - Namuh's friend from birth that epitomizes the timid soul living in fear.

Divine Self-Expression - The supreme Law of which the 13 Universal Laws are interconnected parts.

Dogma - Doctrines and creeds formed by the organizations promoting a limited interpretation of sacred writings. They are the accumulated thoughts, conclusions and traditions of religious leaders that become the accepted understanding of a truth.

Ecnadnuba (Nuba) - Nuba is the team member who stresses the abundance that has always been available to the Nam and the fact that the problem had always been in the minds of the Nam. Both abundance and shortages are created by the way we think.

Efil - The name used by Renni Nam to stress that God is life, the force within all matter.

Twelve Commandments - The points that the priest caste chose to emphasize from their perversion of the instructions recorded in the Captain's Log.

Eveileb (Eve) and Wonk – Eve and Wonk are the team members that relate their story stressing the importance of knowing and believing. Their point is that both are necessary and ineffective without the other.

Elijah - The prophet who in the Hebrew text was taken up into heaven in a flying vehicle that obviously glowed or had an afterburner that could be observed from the ground. The description "fiery chariot" was the only point of reference the observer could possibly have had.

Evig - The team member, who in conversation with Namuh, pointed out the importance of giving and pointed the way to Namuh's understanding of this Universal Law.

Erup Laitentop - The team member who pointed out the pure potentiality of the Nam which begins with thought. The creative process begins here because without thought there can be no form.

Etaler - The team member who stressed his understanding of how all is related to all.

Etam - The name I gave to the wife of Namuh.

Evitcepsrep (Evit) - The team member who revealed to Namuh the importance of proper perspective.

Evol - The one seen as mother of the house that Namuh built. She stresses the importance of love, which is the glue that connects the Universal Laws.

Felieb - the vegetable grown in the individual gardens of the Nam people which when taken with Wonk, constituted a complete diet. When the Nam people had both Felieb and Wonk they were said to have Mod or be blest.

Fles Tseretni - The team member whose experience reveals understanding of the Law of Righteous Self-Interest and its connection to the Law of Giving.

Gnieb - The member who recognizes and discusses the Law of Being with Namuh.

Great Bird, The - The descriptive name given to the plane in which the pilot and his crew had come to the valley.

Great God Pilot, The - This is the sacred name of God as it was understood to be by the Crew Elders. The source was the Captain's log.

Hebrew God - Reference is made to the Hebrew God in the Old Testament scriptures, which are the revelation of the God of the Hebrews.

Holey House - The derogatory description of the house that Namuh built. It was meant to make fun of what they perceived to be a hole in the roof and the fact that Namuh believed the house would be the holy place of God.

Hturt - The son of Namuh.

I AM - This is one of the descriptions of God found in the teachings of the Great Masters

Infallibility - The state of being unable to make a mistake.

King Tnetopmi - In the story he epitomizes impotency. He has the title but no power and in fact can do little or nothing for the people.

Law of the Log, The - The source of the laws developed by the priest was the Captain's Log. The interpretation was developed due to their limited understanding and the awe with which the crew were held.

Levels of the Mind - The house that Namuh built represented the mind of man and therefore the seven levels of the mind. These levels of mind are described in the story.

Manifest - The physical result of creation in thought.

Missile - The name given to the evil one or the one they supposed was an enemy of the god who had come to the valley.

Mission - It comes from the captain's Log and came to mean for the Nam their purpose in life or their job assignment.

Mod - The abbreviated name for Modsiw, the state of fullness or completeness, used in the Nam greetings. It represents wisdom.

Nam - The word I chose to represent the people of the valley.

Namuh - The name of the central figure in the story. He represents the unfoldment of the human mind.

Namuh's House - In the story, it is the house that Namuh believes he has been instructed to build for God. My model is a silo.

Navigator, The - Because in the Captain's Log, the Navigator was designated as second in command behind the pilot and the one responsible for the direction the plane was to take, it was the title chosen for the Chief Priest as the highest authority after God himself.

"No Nam" - To be declared a "No Nam" was essentially to say one was not a man, not human or did not exist as far as the people of Nam were concerned - It was their term for banishment.

Pacification - In the story it is used in the same way as it was used by the Spanish conquerors of Latin America. The people were to be used for the greater glory of God. The crew of the aircraft, which had come to the valley were to control and develop a working unit for the benefit of the mission for which they were present. It was not to please and pacify the people of the valley but to control and utilize their resources.

Queen Yhtapa - In the story she represents apathy.

Raef - The heir apparent to the aging Chief Priest. He represents the brooding danger of fear, our greatest enemy.

Regna - The wife of Raef - She represents the result of fear and that is unreasoning anger.

Renni Nam - The name I gave to the Sage who taught Universal Truths and was banished for his trouble. He represents the teacher within us. His presence, like our inner

Being, is present but shut out. He watches but to gain from him we have to go within Self.

Self - The Being within each individual that is the essence of that life.

Speaker Within, The - The term Renni Nam uses for the source of knowledge that Namuh received in his visitation from God.

Spring - While winter in the story represents chaos and the state in which many perceive the world to exist. Spring is the orderly unfoldment of the human mind. It represents a new beginning, an explosion of life or the expression of God, the life force. It is the birth of awareness.

Tcartta (Cartta) - The team member who recognizes the Universal Law of Attraction and talks about it with Namuh.

Theocracy - A government controlled by religious dogma. A system of governance based on religion as opposed to secular rules.

Truth - Freedom from fear

Universal Law - The thirteen universal principles that Namuh discovers with his unfoldment. These are the 13 Universal Truths as revealed by the Great Masters such a Jesus and Buddha.

Universal Being - This is the primary name for God used by Renni Nam to explain the nature of God. He had earlier used the name Efil, representing the life force within all living beings

Universal Truths - This is another name for Universal Laws and the principles upon which all laws are based.

Valley of the Nam - The valley represents earth, the habitat of man.

Winter - The winter in the story represents chaos, the uncontrolled elements. It is the lack of order in which many philosophers and even scientists today think man lives. It is the reverse of order that the Universal Laws testify to, but even chaos is part of the order.

Wonk - the abbreviation for Egdelwonk, the staple crop of the Nam people. In the language of the mind, food is the taking in of knowledge and in the book represents knowledge. Also the name of Eveileb's husband.

Worran - The Chief Priest, who in the story, is the equivalent of the earthly leader ordained by God. He is depicted as comfortable only with a strict interpretation of the law.

Ynomrah - The young daughter of Namuh. She represents harmony in Namuh's family.

Ytinu - The team member that shows understanding of the absolute unity of all.

Renford

THE RENFORD BOOKS

The course of study provided by the Institute of Applied Metaphysics utilizes all ten of the Renford Books. The lessons are taken from chapters in these books. The glossaries in each book are very important and should not be overlooked

The Universal Laws

This book identifies thirteen Universal Laws that were taught by the Great Masters. The emphasis is on how their teachings were alike as opposed to how they were different. Readers and students can see for themselves how the original teachings parallel each other. In the process, what has been added can be identified.

Universal Being vs. The Father Confusors

This is a study of ancient scripture and the parallels that can be seen in related stories. It is the second phase of the study program and builds on the lessons learned from *The Universal Laws*. Once the Universal Laws are understood, at least on a basic level, *Universal Being vs. The Father Confusors* helps differentiate between Universal Being and entities that were thought to be God or posed as God. The First Cause, The Creative Force we call God, is identified through the Divine Self-Expression, the Universal Laws.

The Metaphysical Bible

Popular and familiar passages such as Isaiah 55, the Lord's Prayer, the 23rd Psalm and others are revealed in a different light. The deeper and, with all due respect to theologians and philosophers, clearer picture of what was being said is recorded for your study. Some, if not all, of the passages interpreted in this book can be found in various books by Renford. In *The Metaphysical Bible*, all are together and in an easily understandable order.

In Search of Self

This is a book of verse by Renford that parallels the other books. In the study of the Universal Laws, you will find that one of these Laws states that to truly understand anything one must experience it personally. *In Search of Self* is the rendering of the Laws in a different way to allow the opportunity for the thoughts of Renford to key off memories of how the Laws have been in play in your own life experiences.

What Now? Essays by Renford

Included in this book is a series of essays by Renford on a variety of subjects of contemporary interest. Always, even though the subject matter is of present day concern, the power and harmony that can be gained by understanding of the ancient teaching of Universal Laws are illustrated.

The Laws of Material Wealth

This book was written for those who are considering career changes or contemplating going into business for themselves. It applies Renford's understanding of the Universal Laws with his experience working with entrepreneurs, especially in start up situations.

The River of Life

Written in prose, this is the story of one Being's awakening to his eternal nature and purpose. The subject of life before and after life is addressed along with the general teachings prevalent concerning rebirth or reincarnation.

The Mysteries Revealed

This is the book Renford never expected to write. It is a metaphysical interpretation of the Book of Revelation. Though most consider it a book of riddles, Revelation is a roadmap to Self unfoldment. It is the mysteries revealed.

The Rules of the Game

The Rules of the Game introduces the Universal Laws in the simplest manner possible. It is not an in-depth study, but provides a basis for understanding of the Laws and the Renford Books. This booklet is analogous to the game of football and the quotes illustrate that even on the simplest everyday matters of life, the Universal Laws are in play.

Renford

THE COURSE OF STUDY

Few will agree with everything in the Renford Books, but it will appeal to those who have come to the conclusion that neither Religion, Science nor technology has all the answers to the origin, nature and future of man.

Understand please that agreement with the Renford Books is not required. The Laws are stated as he came to understand them. You may or may not, in time, come to understand them in the same manner.

There are many who have been unable to reconcile the nature of the petulant and often murderous god of the Old Testament with the loving Father as revealed in the New Testament by Jesus. The Biblical accounts often sound like fairy stories or the ravings of a lunatic fringe, yet contain undeniable truths. The enigmas of the Bible have always perplexed man. The Renford Books give clear and logical explanations, which reveal, clarify and uplift.

Science has given us many answers, but even those who profess to deal only in hard facts cannot completely string all these hard facts together into a rational explanation. Science Fiction writers who extrapolate many seemingly unanswerable questions into plausible explanations also come up short when they try to give some meaning to events.

A bewildering array of philosophical writings have attempted to answer the great questions. "Why are we here? How did we come to be here at this moment in time and under these circumstances? What is the purpose of it all?" These are the perennial questions to which for many there appear to be no

143

answers. In the midst of it all, we can say that we believe this or that principle to be true but we want to **know** if they are.

There are things in the sacred writings that may not seem to ring true, but this is also the case with Science. Once the scientist gets past concrete facts his theories are just as esoteric as the mystic. There are facts proven by Science yet where the question of "why" appears, there is a huge void. This is because Science can only study the manifested reality of thought and not the force that creates the thought.

This course is for those who have logically concluded that the answers are not the special property of any party or discipline. When one finally comes to the conclusion that this universe, the earth and man could have been influenced by a variety of sources and that there may be truths hidden among the wreckage strewn by developing man, it can be said that the eyes are open for the search. Renford says, "It is possible to discern the outline of truth simply by reading ancient text with eyes open."

Before we can play any kind of game, we must learn the rules. What are the laws governing this game of life? These are great questions which have plagued man from his entry into the game, that is from the point in time he identified himself as different from animals, a thinking being. Do we operate in a great vacuum of chaos with our being subject to chance? If there is no reason behind it all, one must conclude there is no supreme mind to give it reason. If reason exists, it follows there must be mind behind it.

Since Science makes no attempt to give us an answer as to what came before the last answer they were able to deduce, the Renford Books go to those who with confidence told us that they had the answers. Unfortunately, what these Great Masters have told us has not just been shrouded in mystery but covered with layers of misunderstanding and even lies.

The questions loom so great that philosophers have felt inadequate to the task. They have picked away at the answers happy to expound a single truth while the minions of organized religion screamed for faith. The Church fathers have maintained that there are unknowable mysteries and that salvation may be found in believing only. These voices throughout history have fought scientific advancement every step of the way. As Science has gained in credibility we have created a new priesthood. This priesthood of scientists has become even more exclusive and condescending than the former.

There is now, and there has always been, but one source for this knowledge. The Universal Truths have always existed. There have been those from the beginning who understood, but it was not then, nor is it now, possible to take in what we are incapable of understanding. Therefore, the knowledge has been preserved or hidden in the open from man. He carries that knowledge within himself, and when he has prepared his container to hold the volume, he has been able to receive it.

This course is designed for those who are prepared to expand their container. Renford has gone to the authoritative sources who gave us the answers. His purpose was to determine what the Universal Laws were, and he reveals that they are the powers that provide the structure we know as life.

The first section of the course reveals and explains the common truths taught by all the great masters. The second section is dedicated to various ancient texts including Biblical accounts. Read with an open mind it is possible to know what is really being revealed. Finally, the third section analyzes the results caused by the "Father Confusors" who came after the Great Masters. They, like those today who have a vested interest in maintaining the present structure, were more interested in showing us their exclusivity and dividing our loyalties than revealing truths.

If tradition and preconceived ideas can be placed in a safe compartment for you to again retreat to, should you find this course too disconcerting, there will be much to be gained by the revelation of truth. Jesus said you will know the truth, and the truth will set you free.

Inquiries with regard to the course can be made by contacting the Institute of Applied Metaphysics at:

3053 Dumbarton Road
Memphis, TN 38128
TL: 901-358-2226
E-mail: information@IAM-CAMPUS.ORG
www.IAM-CAMPUS.ORG

ABOUT THE AUTHOR

Renford has been a life long student of the Bible. The eldest son of a Christian minister, he trained for the ministry and served as a missionary teacher in South Viet Nam during the war.

In his search for common ground with his students, he became a student of Eastern religions and philosophy. Where he had been taught to look for the differences and evangelize lost souls, his studies led him to the conclusion that there were certain principles common to all religions. This book and all of his works pertain to the Universal Laws, which have been in existence before matter and time began.

Renford remained abroad for 20 years, living and working in the Far East, the Middle East and Europe. His books strike to the heart of religion and philosophy - the original principles taught by all the Great Masters. Each book deals with how they are alike as opposed to how they are different. He maintains the differences came about due to the organization builders who came after the Great Masters.

Using a sports analogy, he says, "One can be taught to tackle, run with the ball, block, and in general perform the functions required to play the game of football but the game cannot exist without the rules. Such a game would not be football. Without first the Laws there could have been no creation and life could not be sustained. The Laws of Life had to exist first because without them, no life would be possible. They are the Divine Self-Expression." He goes on to say, "Understand the rules of the game of life and it is possible to be in harmony and find purpose in it.

Printed in the United States
928700003B